More Praise for *Church Turned Inside Out*

"This book was incubated over decades of trench work— observing, questioning, thinking, and synthesizing. In profound and gracious ways, Linda Bergquist and Allan Karr expose church design flaws, fuzzy thinking, and systemic blind spots. As coaches they insist on freedom to create the future; they celebrate distinctiveness; and they bring a practitioner's clarity about the process of great church design. . . . Far from simplistic, this highly accessible book will ignite your imagination for what Christ's church can be in our complex and ever-shifting culture."

—**Carol Davis,** cofounder, catalyst,
coach, LeafLine Initiatives

"This brilliant book speaks wisely and uniquely on so many levels—artistically, intellectually and practically— to the current church planting scene. I highly recommend it. . . . *Church Turned Inside Out* is a concise and poignant guide to starting churches in this new century."

—**Andrew Jones,** mission catalyst, Church Mission
Society; director, the Boaz Project

"Linda and Allan give us practical and theologically innovative tools for rethinking church from an inside-out, upside-down, backward-forward approach. They challenge us with a clean slate that is Christ-focused for building an effective church model by taking us several steps backward before strategy, before values, before vision, and even before mission to identity."

—**Margaret Slusher,** president, LeadPlus

CHURCH TURNED
INSIDE OUT

A GUIDE FOR DESIGNERS, REFINERS, AND RE-ALIGNERS

Linda Bergquist and Allan Karr

FOREWORD BY ALAN HIRSCH

A LEADERSHIP ⁜ NETWORK PUBLICATION

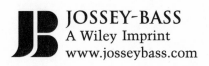

JOSSEY-BASS
A Wiley Imprint
www.josseybass.com

Published by Jossey-Bass
A Wiley Imprint
989 Market Street, San Francisco, CA 94103-1741—www.josseybass.com

Jossey-Bass books and products are available through most bookstores. To contact Jossey-Bass directly call our Customer Care Department within the U.S. at 800-956-7739, outside the U.S. at 317-572-3986, or fax 317-572-4002.

Jossey-Bass also publishes its books in a variety of electronic formats. Some content that appears in print may not be available in electronic books.

All scripture quotations, unless otherwise indicated, are taken from the HOLY BIBLE, NEW INTERNATIONAL VERSION®. NIV®. Copyright© 1973, 1978, 1984 by International Bible Society. Used by permission of Zondervan. All rights reserved.

Library of Congress Cataloging-in-Publication Data
Bergquist, Linda, date.
    Church turned inside out: a guide for designers, refiners, and re-aligners/Linda Bergquist and Allan Karr.
        p.   cm.
    Includes bibliographical references and index.
    ISBN 978-0-470-38317-9 (cloth)
        1. Church renewal. l. Karr, Allan, 1963- II. Title.
    BV600.3.B47 2010
    254'.5—dc22
                                                                            200902342

Printed in the United States of America

FIRST EDITION
HB Printing   10 9 8 7 6 5 4 3 2 1

LEADERSHIP NETWORK TITLES

The Blogging Church: Sharing the Story of Your Church Through Blogs, Brian Bailey and Terry Storch

Church Turned Inside Out: A Guide for Designers, Refiners, and Re-Aligners, Linda Bergquist and Allan Karr

Leading from the Second Chair: Serving Your Church, Fulfilling Your Role, and Realizing Your Dreams, Mike Bonem and Roger Patterson

The Way of Jesus: A Journey of Freedom for Pilgrims and Wanderers, Jonathan S. Campbell with Jennifer Campbell

Leading the Team-Based Church: How Pastors and Church Staffs Can Grow Together into a Powerful Fellowship of Leaders, George Cladis

Church 3.0: Upgrades for the Future of the Church, Neil Cole

Organic Church: Growing Faith Where Life Happens, Neil Cole

Off-Road Disciplines: Spiritual Adventures of Missional Leaders, Earl Creps

Reverse Mentoring: How Young Leaders Can Transform the Church and Why We Should Let Them, Earl Creps

Building a Healthy Multi-Ethnic Church: Mandate, Commitments, and Practices of a Diverse Congregation, Mark DeYmaz

Leading Congregational Change Workbook, James H. Furr, Mike Bonem, and Jim Herrington

The Tangible Kingdom: Creating Incarnational Community, Hugh Halter and Matt Smay

Leading Congregational Change: A Practical Guide for the Transformational Journey, Jim Herrington, Mike Bonem, and James H. Furr

The Leader's Journey: Accepting the Call to Personal and Congregational Transformation, Jim Herrington, Robert Creech, and Trisha Taylor

Whole Church: Leading from Fragmentation to Engagement, Mel Lawrenz

Culture Shift: Transforming Your Church from the Inside Out, Robert Lewis and Wayne Cordeiro, with Warren Bird

Church Unique: How Missional Leaders Cast Vision, Capture Culture, and Create Movement, Will Mancini

A New Kind of Christian: A Tale of Two Friends on a Spiritual Journey, Brian D. McLaren

The Story We Find Ourselves In: Further Adventures of a New Kind of Christian, Brian D. McLaren

Missional Renaissance: Changing the Scorecard for the Church, Reggie McNeal

Practicing Greatness: 7 Disciplines of Extraordinary Spiritual Leaders, Reggie McNeal

The Present Future: Six Tough Questions for the Church, Reggie McNeal

A Work of Heart: Understanding How God Shapes Spiritual Leaders, Reggie McNeal

The Millennium Matrix: Reclaiming the Past, Reframing the Future of the Church, M. Rex Miller

Shaped by God's Heart: The Passion and Practices of Missional Churches, Milfred Minatrea

Missional Map-Making: Skills for Leading in Times of Transition, Alan J. Roxburgh

The Missional Leader: Equipping Your Church to Reach a Changing World, Alan J. Roxburgh and Fred Romanuk

Relational Intelligence: How Leaders Can Expand Their Influence Through a New Way of Being Smart, Steve Saccone

Becoming an Externally Focused Church: A Practical Guide for the Transformational Journey, Eric Swanson and Rick Rusaw

The Ascent of a Leader: How Ordinary Relationships Develop Extraordinary Character and Influence, Bill Thrall, Bruce McNicol, and Ken McElrath

Beyond Megachurch Myths: What We Can Learn from America's Largest Churches, Scott Thumma and Dave Travis

The Elephant in the Boardroom: Speaking the Unspoken About Pastoral Transitions, Carolyn Weese and J. Russell Crabtree

CONTENTS

FIGURES AND TABLES

ABOUT LEADERSHIP NETWORK

Since 1984, Leadership Network has fostered church innovation and growth by diligently pursuing its far-reaching mission statement: to identify, connect, and help high-capacity Christian leaders multiply their impact.

Although Leadership Network's techniques adapt and change as the church faces new opportunities and challenges, the organization's work follows a consistent and proven pattern: Leadership Network brings together entrepreneurial leaders who are focused on similar ministry initiatives. The ensuing collaboration—often across denominational lines—creates a strong base from which individual leaders can better analyze and refine their own strategies. Peer-to-peer interaction, dialogue, and sharing inevitably accelerate participants' innovation and ideas. Leadership Network further enhances this process through developing and distributing highly targeted ministry tools and resources, including audio and video programs, special reports, e-publications, and online downloads.

With Leadership Network's assistance, today's Christian leaders are energized, equipped, inspired, and better able to multiply their own dynamic Kingdom-building initiatives.

Launched in 1996 in conjunction with Jossey-Bass (a Wiley imprint), Leadership Network Publications present thoroughly researched and innovative concepts from leading thinkers, practitioners, and pioneering churches. The series collectively draws from a range of disciplines, with individual titles offering perspective on one or more of five primary areas:

1. Enabling effective leadership
2. Encouraging life-changing service
3. Building authentic community
4. Creating Kingdom-centered impact
5. Engaging cultural and demographic realities

For additional information on the mission or activities of Leadership Network, please contact:

Leadership Network
(800) 765-5323
client.care@leadnet.org

FOREWORD

by Alan Hirsch

Mission, by its very nature, calls us into risky engagement, and because it does that it requires constant vigilance, relearning, adaptation, and unrelenting adjustments in the life of the organization. Therefore, missional church (the church that organizes itself around the mission of God in the world) by its very definition must call into question many of the inherited ideas that underpin the prevailing forms and ideas of church. If left unchallenged, institutionalized dimensions of church life will inevitably pull the church into a vortex that will not only suppress the message but in the process destroy the spiritual legitimacy of the church itself. Emil Brunner was right: the church does exist by its mission—we are a message tribe, after all. So, if the church's built-in missional impulse fails to challenge the status quo, progress itself would be impossible. The biblical teaching on the Kingdom of God is predicated on the idea that we have not yet reached the ideal yet. The best is yet to come, and we must all lean into the task of participating in God's dreams and desires for our world. There is much work to be done, and much of it involves change.

However, we would be less than biblical if we were to do this work divorced from a lively sense of theology, history, and tradition. Our very identity, our culture, our worldview are formed by the stories that have shaped, sustained, and enabled us to get to this very point in time. History and tradition are important guides to genuinely *biblical* thinking. To find this balance between the conservative forces of tradition and the progressive forces of mission is as rare as it is difficult, because by nature the imposing Kingdom demands constant repentance while our living sense of identity requires remembrance and conservation of the ideas and events that have shaped us.

This being said, both Linda Bergquist and Allan Karr do precisely that; they are radical traditionalists. They play out their vision of the church right at the intersection where the future meets the past in the present, and in so doing they challenge the status quo of contemporary forms of church while at the same time being very respectful of its relative successes and the faithfulness of our evangelical tradition.

Most churches in the evangelical wing of the church sincerely long to have an impact on their world, but they are somehow stuck in the same systems story that binds them to past practices. I believe the strategic battle for the mission of the church in our time will be won or lost at the level of imagination. It is a matter of how we conceive the church, of what image of the church dominates our thinking. If we fail to get to reconceive the church *missionally,* then we can expect more of the same (diminishing) results that we are currently achieving. What I like about this book is that it is not just about *good ole* American pragmatism. It blends theology, biblical imagery, and metaphors from culture and creation to offer up a fertile vision of what the church must become; it provides respectful ways to look at adaptation and change. This is a book that will help mainstream evangelicals move forward to their own next steps and nurture leaders who find themselves yearning to be more faithful to the missional cause of Jesus' church.

Both authors have long-term experience in guiding established churches as well as in church planting and networking. They are missiologists, theologians, and practitioners, and it is the combination of these ministries that legitimizes what they say. As far as I am concerned, this is a well-researched, genuinely intelligent, missiologically fertile book—and a good piece of writing to boot. It is a valuable addition to the newly burgeoning assortment of books on missional church.

Well done, Linda and Allan. May God bless and use this work.

Alan Hirsch is the author of *The Forgotten Ways, reJesus,* and *The Shaping of Things to Come;* the founder of Forge Missional Training Network; and cofounder of shapevine.com.

To Kathy
My patient and faithful partner in the journey,
Who inspires us all daily with encouragement—Allan

To Fred Jappe
My friend and teacher,
Who first introduced me to the living Christ—Linda

PREFACE

This is a design book. It is also an ecology book, a philosophy book, an organizational book, an art book, and a church book—with a little biology, mathematics, physics, and history thrown in. Why not? It seems like a good way for churches to reflect the never-changing, ever-transforming, all-knowing nature of God. One reason we chose to write from the perspective of multiple disciplines is that it is something we as authors simply enjoy doing. Learning from many arenas of God's world is part of what it means for us to "delight in the Lord."

A story from the life of Henry Ford helped inform the direction of this book. Ford reinvented transportation by designing an efficient, lightweight engine that made automobiles affordable. Always a populist, he wanted all his factory workers to be able to own a car. His innovative ideas about mass production catapulted his dream to such an extent that at one point the Ford Motor Company manufactured more than half of the automobiles on American roads. Perhaps Ford's most unique idea, however, was to share the profits with the employees. On January 11, 1914, the *New York Times* reported the "good to great" story of Ford's journey to fame. The headline that day read: "Henry Ford Explains Why He Gives Away $10,000,000; Declares That He Is Dividing Profits with His Employees, Not Paying Them Higher Wages, and That Workers as Partners Will Give Increased Efficiency."[1] As amazing as Ford was in both product and process innovation, he also had his blind spots. In his autobiography he wrote, "In the future we were going to build only one model, that the model was going to be 'Model T,' and that the chassis would be exactly the same for all cars."[2] Ford added: "Any customer can have a car painted any color that he wants so long as it is black."[3] Ford was so focused on his goal of reproducing cars for the masses that he made an intentional decision not to be innovative in other arenas of automobile production.

Sometimes, Christians think that only our own brand of "Model T church" ought to be produced. Sometimes we are so focused on mass production of new churches and new Christians that, in the name of biblical reproduction, we forget that God doesn't paint in just one color. Not everyone agreed with Henry Ford, and of course eventually the Ford Motor Company produced hundreds of kinds of cars. This book invites readers to think like designers, and remain open to many new kinds of expression of the body of Christ.

We have taught and lived the content of this book for years but never thought to write about what we learned. Two stories (one from Allan and one from Linda) served as a-ha moments that led us to record our experiences. Allan calls his story the "Zwingli Crisis." It happened in Switzerland while Allan, his family, and some students were visiting church planter Corey Best and assisting him with the new church there. One day, the group visited Grossmünster, a historic church in Zurich where the sixteenth-century reformer Ulrich Zwingli was once pastor. A tour guide introduced them to a side of Zwingli they never knew.

Apparently Zwingli opposed nearly everyone: the Catholic Church of Switzerland, which he sought to demolish; his contemporary, Martin Luther; and the radical reformers, who included his former students. He was particularly incensed by two of his own students, Conrad Grebel and Felix Manz, who believed that the Bible taught believer baptism rather than infant Baptism, and as a result he presided over the death of several of them. Even though Zwingli helped initiate change in Switzerland, he frequently persecuted those who disagreed with him. The power structures Zwingli represented could not accommodate the designers, refiners, and re-aligners of his own day. Allan decided he didn't like Zwingli very much, and the experience served to ignite in him a passion to help the next generation of leaders find their place in the new story of what God is doing in the world today. The episode and its outcome eventually led toward this book.

Linda's a-ha experience happened when her daughter, Kristina, became a student at San Francisco's Lick-Wilmerding High School (LWHS), which calls itself a "private school with a public purpose." Every year, LWHS selects a group of incoming students not only on the basis of individual strengths but also on how the group seems to form some kind of diverse and balanced whole. After selecting students, the school works with families and extends scholarships, as needed, from its endowment fund. Tuition includes everything, so that families who send their children to LWHS do not have to plan for any additional expenses, and every student is able to participate in all activities. Not only that, but families are invited into the life of the school. As part of a first-semester family, Linda was invited to co-chair a major committee, not because of social connections or wealth (her daughter received generous financial aid from the school), but because of her prior experience.

Education at LWHS means learning to use head, heart, and hands for a greater good. Students and faculty alike are deeply involved in the life of the community. The school began the Lick-Wilmerding Center for Civic Engagement, which "marshals and leverages our community's knowledge, networks and resources to benefit the common good. We do so, in part, by creating meaningful service learning opportunities and convening service-related conversations among teachers and students at LWHS and across the country."[4]

The school began one program to help tutor urban middle school children and another to give scholarships to high school children from less advantaged schools. It also initiated a learning service project with a destitute school in Senegal, and more. Everything from the green architecture to the unique learning experiences resonates fully with Lick Wilmerding's values and beliefs. LWHS is a beautifully designed organization, much like the beautifully designed churches that Linda imagines.

Although we have taught the content of *Church Turned Inside Out* for years, writing it down made it fresh again. Everything, like these two stories, became an incredible new learning experience that helped us think differently as well as care differently. In some ways, though, this book found us along the way. We thought we knew how its story would end, but it is really still unfolding. Many ideas surfaced that, until now, we had been content to keep tucked away in our minds. We may have never dusted them off, but that seemed too indulgent. Some of those ideas were never spoken aloud except between us as coauthors. They seemed raw and new, even to us. We also knew God was shaping us through many people in our lives, but we didn't realize how many there were and how deeply we love and appreciate them.

Additionally, we thought we understood teamwork. After all, we both teach about it; but one of the great experiences of writing this book was the teamship we learned to share with one another. Through this process, we discovered more about our own selves and about what it meant to value and appreciate one another. In many ways, we are quite opposite, with different genders, ages, writing and work styles, thought processes, personalities, and spiritual gifts. Neither of us could have written nearly as well without the other because it took both of us to make this book complete. But as you read *Church Turned Inside Out,* you will discover that, in the end, learning and being together is what it's all about.

CHURCH TURNED
INSIDE OUT

1

THE ONCE AND FUTURE CHURCH

"That's the effect of living backwards," the Queen said kindly: "it always makes one a little giddy at first—"

"Living backwards!" Alice repeated in great astonishment. "I never heard of such a thing!"

"—but there's one great advantage in it, that one's memory works both ways."

"I'm sure mine only works one way," Alice remarked. "I can't remember things before they happen."

"It's a poor sort of memory that only works backwards," the Queen remarked.
—LEWIS CARROLL, *ALICE IN WONDERLAND*[1]

THIS IS A BOOK ABOUT DESIGN. It is about conceiving, birthing, and conceptualizing. It is also about experience and emotional attachment, utility, and appreciation. The chair that you love is comfortable and good for your back. It is well suited for the particular space you call home, and it is uniquely your own. It serves your mission of relaxing in the evening while you read or watch television. Whether your spouse agrees or not, this chair is your own designer original.

The idea of design in this book takes in all of these kinds of ideas. In some ways, you might call it "interior design" because we start with the inside (you, your beliefs, and your values). This is the exact opposite of how many people use the word *design* because they think design is about outer appearances, like making something pretty or giving it a finishing touch. In the church world, there is a great tendency to improve or fix things on the outside by adding or subtracting various programs or methodologies. Here, the process is reversed and intentionally more systemic. It introduces the church to a whole new design experiment.

In 1803, after negotiating the Louisiana Purchase, Thomas Jefferson commissioned Meriwether Lewis and William Clark to lead an expedition to explore the newly annexed territory. The president was hoping to discover the existence of a waterway to the west coast. With no roads and no maps, the expedition, known as the Corps of Discovery, had to work from the inside out, creating something where nothing they knew about already existed. They forged a crude route from Saint Louis to the Pacific, returning two years later. When they began, the explorers knew only the path from St. Louis to as far as they could see up the Missouri River, but by the time they finished they had charted a pathway for the United States to span its settlement from ocean to ocean.

Allan often asks his students to consider what it would have been like if Congress had required Lewis and Clark to draw a map of where they were going before they left. What if they had speculated a journey, developed a strategy, and drawn a map based on traveling a waterway nobody knew was actually there? Any plan to adhere to this kind of scheme would have alienated Congress, disheartened the team, and failed hopelessly within days after the expedition began.

As you read this book, we are asking you to abandon your maps and lay aside your preconceived ideas, plans, strategies, and models related to the churches you care about. We want you to think from the inside out, starting with some concepts you may have never considered important. As you move through the chapters, with God's help you will eventually be able to draw a relevant, realistic, and thoughtful kind of map. We believe this will be your experience as a result of having dealt with some new, different, or defining issues.

At the end of the Corps of Discovery, Clark presented Jefferson with a series of amazingly detailed expedition maps that noted rivers, creeks, significant points of interest, and even the shape of shorelines. These maps helped future explorers continue probing the western territory. As you embark on your personal "corps of discovery," we hope you will glean insights on your journey as a church designer, refiner, or re-aligner. Perhaps the maps you draw will also be helpful to future travelers who are preparing to define new territory for God's people.

Amid some of the most rapid change humanity has ever experienced, we have written this book out of a conscious decision to live well in a gap that connects the present to the future. This gap represents the two great tasks for the church in North America today. The first of these is predictable and in the present: the church must do everything it already knows how to do, as sustainably as it can, so that as many people as possible begin to follow Christ obediently, become involved in authentic Christian communities, and multiply disciples. The second great task of the church is oriented toward the future: the church must also commit to the adventure of figuring out how to reach the growing number of people who are resistant to the gospel as it has been expressed in past generations.

The Task of Sustaining the Present

The church knows a lot about reaching people who adhere to a fuzzy faith in God, who already believe that the Bible is true, and who are open to the idea of church, but who need to hear the call of Christ and to make changes in their hearts, attitudes, and behaviors. There are millions who will hear about the four spiritual laws, and learn how to discover steps to peace with God, and how to have an abundant life. Hearing, we hope they will believe, and by believing become involved in a church, live better, and go to heaven when they die.

In many places in North America today, this is still a primary need. The Association of Religion Data Archives shows that more than two-thirds of people in the United States have no doubt that God exists, believe in heaven, and believe that being a Christian is very important or fairly important. In the same survey, only one-third of respondents say they have ever had a born-again experience. Roughly speaking, this means that approximately one-third of all people living in the United States are not born-again Christians but may be quite open to this kind of an encounter with Christ.[2] Others come to know Christ in different ways, such as Ruth Graham, the late wife of America's favorite evangelist, who cannot ever remember a time when she did not feel close to Christ.

Children who grow up in homes where Christ is real, and where parents pray for their daughters and sons, are more likely to follow him when they are old, but those kinds of homes have become rare. San Francisco is one example of a city where there has been a gap in the type of historical Christianity to which we refer. It experienced what is often called postmodernity forty years before most people ever heard of the term. Not realizing what they were up against, local churches retreated and failed to make their practices relevant to the culture in which they found themselves. Most became increasingly ineffective, and many grew weary from trying to implement new methodologies that seemed effective in other American cities but that failed in San Francisco. Decades passed, and San Francisco became a radically unchurched city whose beautiful old church buildings stood nearly empty.

When the Billy Graham Crusade came to San Francisco in the late 1990s, it served more of a seed-sowing purpose than a harvesting purpose. It was a novelty, and perhaps even an honor, that the world-famous evangelist chose San Francisco. However, the crusade did not have an impact on the city or its churches in any real way. Many Christians dismissed it: "Nothing works in the spiritual battlefield of San Francisco. Let's go instead where God is working." Translated, "go where God is working" sometimes means "go to some large, rapidly growing, homogeneous, suburban, preferably politically conservative population base where a congregation can quickly become numerically successful." This misinterpretation of the church growth movement and its principles has left hundreds of thousands of today's urban dwellers without even a memory of a relevant gospel message.

A few years ago on Easter morning, a church planter named John sat outside a community center in the Haight district of San Francisco, which forty years earlier was the center of the Jesus Movement. John seized the quiet moment, and strummed his guitar as he worshipped God. A neighbor poked his head out of the four-story house next door. "Come on up here and play some Jesus music for us," the man requested. John obliged, and after a few songs the household asked John a serious question: "Can you tell us what the meaning of Easter is? We've been asking people all week, and nobody remembers."

Nobody remembers the meaning of Easter! The present-day task of the church is clear. Christians must continue to do everything they already know how to do to reach the most receptive people, now in places in North America that still hold historically positive images of Church.

The Task of Addressing the Future

Because the number of those who simply need the gospel story clarified and committed to heart before coming to Christ is fewer than we dare realize, the second great task is very important. A growing number of North Americans are not at all responsive to the story the way we have learned to share it. They do not believe that the Bible is true, or even useful. In their worldview, it is important that a spiritual tradition be able to help people know how to live together on the planet in such a way that we do not destroy one another, and do not destroy the prospects of future generations. They see Christianity, in its seeming exclusivity—with its core belief that the only way to God is through Jesus—as more detrimental than helpful in seeking these global outcomes. It seems there is no acceptable place in this new world for people who believe their group alone has a corner on truth, or who try to enlist others to believe and practice as they do (evangelism).

Others simply find the Christian story archaic and irrelevant. They wonder why we persist in taking our old Book so seriously. They could care less whether humans are saved by grace or by good works. In the midst of this upheaval, we find this second great challenge of the church in North America today. The church must learn to be and do what it does not already know. With all of our hearts, we must address the future together.

It is said that Beethoven, who was a wildly successful musician in his own day, began at one point in his career writing pieces that were so unlike his previous works that his friends were astonished and asked, "Ludwig, what's happened to you? We don't understand you anymore!" According to the story, Beethoven, with a studied sweep of the hand, replied, "I have said all I have to say to my contemporaries; now I am speaking to the future." His later works, including his Ninth Symphony and the string quartet

Grosse Fuge, became some of the most important musical pieces ever composed.[3]

Our aim is similar. We wish to speak to the future. We hope to slow down the depletion of the church's present assets so that they do not become tomorrow's liabilities too quickly. We also want to help future perspectives become present practices in authentic, practical ways. We must ask ourselves what is here for the long haul, and what needs an overhaul or a reconstruction. We will be talking about design, as a process and mind-set that can help everyone who cares about these issues of present and future move forward. Our design process turns thinking processes upside down and inside out. Our readers should not be surprised by such an approach, though we imagine that it will irritate some in the same way that Jesus irritated religious leaders with His countercultural, inside-out ideas: to be rich you must be poor; to be first, you must be last; to live you must first die; to gain you must lose; and it is by giving that you receive.

"Inside-out" thinking is what we are after. We hope to help our readers think about church in ways that are good for them and the people they lead. Designers do not start with existing models and paradigms, and neither will we. Instead we begin on the inside, with you and the people who are journeying with you, and we work our way outward toward a paradigm or way of understanding church. Our approach is both reconciliatory and revolutionary and does not necessarily mean starting over; nor does it require disassociation with historic faith. In his book *Retrieving the Tradition and Renewing Evangelicalism: A Primer for Suspicious Protestants,* Daniel Williams describes the disconnect between the contemporary church and historical faith traditions as "amnesia." He says that the real problem with amnesia is that "not only do you forget your loved ones, but no longer remember who you are."[4] It is possible to love and respect the church even while calling for change.

Here is a picture of what we mean. When the Bergquist family purchased their 1931 Mediterranean home, it came with a classic bright pink and black tiled bathroom. If they had built the house themselves, they would have chosen some other tile and designed the bathroom differently (design). If enough money were available, they would have made several remodeling decisions, including finding old authentic replacement tile in another color (re-align).

With neither available, they opted to accessorize with complementary modern colors (refine). The result is that they were able to find a way to integrate colors and style so that the look is both contemporary and classic, respecting both the home's character and the Bergquists' tastes. Nothing about it seems either mass produced or unintentional.

McChurch or Mac Church?

McDonald's and Apple are household names. Their products, such as Big Macs and Macintosh computers, are iconic representations of America's success. Although some may prefer the two not be mentioned in the same breath, there are actually a number of similarities in the corporate cultures of these industry giants. Both are fast-paced companies that have their own operating systems. They like to control the entire consumer experience, or what Steve Jobs calls "the whole widget."[5] Both are intentionally rooted in consumer accessibility, and both turn out new products with regularity. However, even though both companies have designed many new products, McDonald's is known as the all-American franchise-in-a-box, while Apple is known for its innovative out-of-the box thinking.

These Mc and Mac stereotypes offer symbolic language for our conversation about church. A few popular models dominate the church landscape. Like McDonald's and Apple, these models have many fans and many critics. A few have worked exceedingly well. They weren't always models; they began with a design. Somebody thought or prayed through a beautifully complete, systemic design process and implemented it faithfully. In our culture, whatever works well is usually imitated, perfected, and reproduced over and over again, often with some predictable rate of success. We're calling this phenomena "McChurch."

In the last few decades, as the church learned to reproduce and perfect certain processes, it has become more effective than ever at reaching the declining number of people who are attracted to existing formats of church. But the church cannot continue to depend on cherry picking forever. To overcome this nonsustainable practice, it is necessary to engage prayerfully in a new missiological orientation that takes design thinking seriously.

This new orientation, which Allan and Linda call "Mac Church," would be different in creating churches with fewer assumptions about how church "ought" to look, what it takes to be effective or productive, and what is good for people's spiritual health. Instead of looking for solutions that fit the masses, it would take individuals' needs and preferences more seriously. The church must learn to do something that is paramount to building an airplane while in flight; it cannot stop what it is already doing to experiment with new approaches. Thus, some must refine and re-align on the basis of already existing models while others, the designers, find ways to radically rethink church.

The Age of Design

Bruce Nussbaum, managing editor in charge of innovation and design coverage at *BusinessWeek*, is acknowledged as one of the world's forty most influential designers. A leading advocate of organizational design for more than twenty years, he calls design thinking the "new Management Methodology," justifying its rising popularity when he says, "There are moments in history when the pace of change is so fast and the shape of the future so fuzzy that we live in a constant state of beta." Nussbaum recognizes the unnecessary tension this brings up: "There is a nice little war going on in the US between those design educators that want to stress strategy and those which focus on form. It's a silly argument to me. Design should not give up its special ability to visualize ideas and give form to options. Design should extend its brief to embrace a more abstract and formalized expression of how it translates empathy to creativity and then to form and experience. . . . Do not deny the powerful problem-solving abilities of design to the cultures of business and society."[6]

The church accepts this same challenge when it not only admits its growing despair in addressing the future but also blesses diverse, God-inspired design attempts to do something about it. In these times of transition, it is imperative for the church's change agents to ask tough questions about the underlying assumptions and mental models that have created the dilemmas we must address. Albert Einstein said problems can't be solved within the mind-set that created them.[7] Even Charlie Brown agreed: "How can you do 'new math' problems with an 'old math' mind?"[8] If they are correct, it is necessary to consider the inside workings of some of our current church systems.

There is a theory that people in systems, including church systems, often have good intentions but end up producing the opposite of what they intend. This phenomenon is being studied in fields as diverse as business, the food industry, education, and medicine, all of which are reexamining their systems in light of a new era of information. In medicine, the term *iatrogenic* is used to refer to conditions or complications that are a result of the treatment, the facilities, or the participants of the healing team. For example, George Washington almost certainly died as a result of a well-intentioned physician draining many pints of his blood rather than supplementing it. Though a customary practice of the day, bloodletting was the tragic opposite of what Washington really needed.

Sarah Mondale and Sarah Patton explored this notion in their PBS film "School: The Story of American Public Education." It seems that early public schools were often built for the children of factory workers. The goal was to create environments that would produce the best possible next generation of factory workers. Public school was the perfect preparation for a structured, bureaucratic society where work was routinized, authority respected, rules obeyed, and where acquisition of basic skills and competencies was more valued than raising up eager learners. The result was a tendency toward broad mediocrity that still infects our public school systems more than one hundred years later.[9]

In a 2005 speech to the National Governor's Association, Microsoft founder Bill Gates said that now "America's high schools are obsolete. By obsolete, I don't just mean that our high schools are broken, flawed, and under-funded—though a case could be made for every one of those points. By obsolete, I mean that our high schools—even when they're working exactly as designed—cannot teach our kids what they need to know today."[10]

Churches founded in this era, during the growth of public education, spread most quickly among people who worked in factories and whose children attended the new public schools. The churches modeled their systems after these same educational organizations. This should not surprise those of us who recognize

that many churches and denominations today learn organizational practices from business organizations. But what if, despite
our good intentions, we are actually propagating church systems
that in our own day are creating the opposite of what we want?

A few years ago, while attending an educational convention,
Linda heard a presenter ask the group a provocative question:
What kind of educational system would we dream up if we were
trying our best to produce people who were not learners? The
answers made her think that people in churches might respond
similarly if they were asked what kind of religious system they
would dream up if they were trying their best to produce people
who did not grow spiritually and if they were trying to create barriers to other people coming to know Christ. She put this question to a class of seminary students. Here are some of the answers
describing such a system:

- The chief activity that people would do together would be
  indoctrination through absorbing information.
- Information gathering would be valued more than practical
  application.
- More attention would be paid to slots in the organization that
  needed to be filled than to the strengthening of people's abilities.
- Participants would be rewarded for agreeing with what they
  were told and punished for exploring new ideas.
- When people met, they would sit silently in straight rows and
  listen to just one person's ideas.
- Language would be created to help distinguish group "insid-
  ers" from those who were outside the group.
- People in the group would spend so much time together
  doing things that helped the system that they would have no
  time left to spend with those outside the system.
- Acceptance would be linked to performance.
- People would be valued for what they contributed to the
  organization and to what they could do to build it up.
- Freethinking would be discouraged, especially asking ques-
  tions considered disloyal.
- Freedom of the press would be eliminated.
- Families would be divided up into activities so that they
  couldn't function as practicing communities during the week.

- People would be valued for what they know more than what they do.
- The message would be that the organization is more important than its people.

When we saw these results we cringed. Ouch! These qualities come a little too close to describing the way a lot of church communities operate, even if they do not necessarily add up to a negative result. Still, it is important to investigate the possibility of our own "illness"-producing practices, and to consider whether our particular traditions of churching are effectively producing the kind of Christian, in the kinds of Christian communities, that most honors our Maker. Although the field of education has spent decades researching and redesigning its systems, the church, in our opinion, has been remiss in finding its own Spirit-led ways to research and design anew.

The title of this book says that it is written for designers, refiners, and re-aligners. This does not necessarily mean that these are three kinds of fixed roles, although some people more easily gravitate to one or the other. The choice is based not only on how individuals are usually called to function as part of the body of Christ but also on the needs of the larger community, the situation, timing, and other considerations. Consider again the Bergquists' pink-and-black bathroom. Their choice to respect the integrity of the old house was not a second-best solution; it was the right one for the situation. Some opportunities call for designing, some call for refining, and some call for re-aligning.

Design is a big word. It encompasses everything from Vera Wang original bridal gowns to mass-produced designer jeans. In some ways, the most exquisite aspects of the design role are open to only the privileged. Just a few can design something new all of the time, and just a few have the luxury of doing so. The church world does not pay for research and development, as pharmaceutical companies do when they are looking for new projects, or government does to explore outer space. The most radical designers in the church world have always paid for their own design processes, either by being judged heretical by their contemporaries, or by being unsuccessful for some period of time before their thoughts form something whole, systemic, and useful. An example is our friend Brad Sargent, a brilliant missiologist designer who has never really found his place. We wish someone could just pay him to think for the rest of his life, and then pay for an army of other people to try a few of his ideas (such as the wonderful quirky learning games he created for students of culture).

The role of the re-aligner is less radical. The re-aligner takes the pieces and makes them fit together in new and better ways. The re-aligner is also a troubleshooter who can spot design flaws. NASA's Genesis space capsule had sensors that were meant to detect deceleration. They were installed correctly but were designed upside down, thus failing to deploy the capsule's parachutes. Because of this design problem, the capsule, which had been carefully collecting solar matter for two years, crashed in the Utah desert in 2004. It would not have crashed if someone had thought to re-align the sensors.

Harold Bullock, founding pastor and inspired designer of Hope Church in Fort Worth, Texas, talks about misalignment in church systems. He starts on the inside with character alignment issues that can eventually make a difference in every aspect of church development. The entire system reflects design integrity because of the emphasis on personal integrity. Harold really believes in good alignment. He says, "you can't put a Volkswagen engine in a Mack truck."[11] In a church design process, there must be a Spirit-led, ongoing alignment that can help forge new directions for the future, keep major efforts from backfiring, and save people from unnecessary pain.

Refining, in the sense of this book, means to improve, perfect, or enrich. Refining is essentially a purification process that is absolutely essential to addressing the future. This is indicated in the story of the man who saw a field and knew beyond the shadow of a doubt that the treasure in the field was so breathtakingly valuable that it was worth selling everything he owned just to buy it (Matt. 13:44).[12] Refiners help us recognize what is valuable when we see it, dig deeply for the treasure, and give up everything to serve it. In this context, refiners call the church to repentance and help rekindle ancient meaning. They prophetically remind pilgrim people to value the Story above the process and the Creator above whatever new thing is created. Sometimes refiners are needed to help hurting churches work through emotional trauma.

They help these churches attain healing and forgiveness, a process that sets them free to re-align around a hopeful future instead of a painful past.

The Design Process

The chapters of this book flow together like tributaries that finally converge. The overarching context for everything we have written is that we believe God is working, speaking, guiding, and informing each arena in ways we can hardly imagine. He is the Master Designer, Re-Aligner, and Refiner. Chapter Two is about acknowledging self. We begin here partly because we sense that "self" is a forgotten place. Churches do mission, start churches, and preach sermons for others, often to the neglect of our own souls. We all forget that God loves us, not just others, and He has a vested interest in seeing us function according to how He wired us. When a baby is born, parents naturally expect that the child's genetic code will show up somewhere. When a church is born and develops, there is no such expectation. But in fact, those who parent churches always bring themselves to the table. This chapter demands that readers be transparent and open about their own selves: to consider and acknowledge their own unique experiences, influences, gifts, talents, and personalities as a first step in thinking through an overall design.

Chapter Three is something like an extension of Chapter Two, but instead of being limited to one individual leader it reflects on communities, bound together in Christ, who live life together and work as a missional team. A single cell is the simplest living thing; however, living things cannot exist alone. Cells exist within the framework or network of other living things. When a cell reproduces, it passes on not only its genes but also its whole cellular network; it is not simply the DNA that reproduces. We suggest too that at this level, a "microcommunity" functions as a unit to carry the genetic code of the church into its larger "macrocommunity." This chapter helps teams consider how their spontaneous friendships, intimacy, shared passion, and interdependencies shape the community and inform design decisions.

Chapters Four and Five are about beliefs. When church planning processes begin with models, methods, and strategies, a set of theological presuppositions and biblical values are often simply assumed, and rarely revisited. Structures, programs, polity, and pragmatics teach theological postures and priorities, whether or not they are ever verbalized. Theology and biblical exegesis may become unintentionally marginalized while pragmatics (whatever works) and social agendas and preferences form the basis for organizational decision making. These chapters ask readers to consider the values and beliefs any church model or structure promotes, and then to make decisions that express their real beliefs and honor God.

In Chapters Six through Eight, we ask readers to consider appropriate ways to engage the larger culture. We challenge you to learn to understand underlying worldviews and to embrace the people to whom you are called. We also want you to ascertain the degree to which you are personally functioning as a cultural insider, or how you are living as missionaries among people whose cultures and worldviews are fundamentally different from your own.

"Without analysis, no synthesis," claimed the German philosopher Eugene Duhring.[13] Our final four chapters are about synthesis. They tie all previous chapters together in away that is supercharged with possibility: What can the church create collectively if it believes that design is more flexible than rigid? First we examine existing models. This section of the book offers a menu of potential existing models, comparing and contrasting them in relationship to the critical factors discussed in earlier chapters such as self, team, culture, beliefs, and values. It dovetails with a chapter about facing tough choices and addressing the consequences of those choices. As a result of reading these chapters, we hope our readers will make fewer design omissions and minimize systemic design flaws.

Finally, the last two chapters consider new ways for churches to think about design. We consider some common metaphors for organizations, and we suggest some practical ways of reorganizing that can help not only designers but re-aligners too. The last chapter of our book is about a whole new way of envisioning organizations. We suggest the possibility of organizing more like living systems than like any classically structured organization.

Einstein said that the world we create is a product of our way of thinking.[14] If so, what kind of world can be created as a result of truly hopeful, inside-out rethinking? How can we think systemically, and open our hearts a little wider? For many years, our journeys have led the two of us in search of the intersection of strategy and Spirit. One place where we have found epiphany is in this concept of systemic, living systems design.

We wrote this book for many reasons. We wrote it because something isn't working, and we don't accept that. We are neither hopeless nor helpless. We wrote it because we yearn for the world to see more clearly the good, just, and sustainable communities of faith that exist all over the planet; but somehow efforts do not translate. We wrote this book because we believe that women and men are created in the image of their Creator to be creative. We long for God's church to experience the freedom that creativity brings from the inside out. We wrote it because we believe in the church and its ordained place in God's plan from the beginning of time.

2

ACKNOWLEDGING SELF

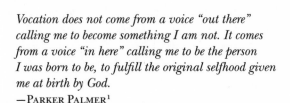

Vocation does not come from a voice "out there"
calling me to become something I am not. It comes
from a voice "in here" calling me to be the person
I was born to be, to fulfill the original selfhood given
me at birth by God.
—PARKER PALMER[1]

BIRDHOUSES, BOOKSHELVES, AND BUILDINGS are constructed similarly. You begin with a plan, assemble tools and components, align the parts according to the plan, and connect them together. Living things do not come together in the same way. Apples, flowers, and fish are grown, not assembled. It is not even true, as most people think, that life happens simply through the division and replication of raw DNA. The genetic code sequences of living things can reproduce only in concert with intricate and explicit life processes that involve entire cellular networks.

Churches are living things, not mechanical. By definition, we are the people of God, the body of Christ, the fellowship of the Spirit. We are "*living* stones . . . being built into a spiritual house to be a holy priesthood."[2] Churches do not come into being by merely aligning the right things or the best resources (leaders, teams, culture, methods, support systems, and right theology). We are called to be like God: code carriers of our Father's identity. To thrive, and ultimately in order to reproduce, we must submit to the life-giving processes of the cellular network, God's church. Christlike DNA carried by individuals (you) in the context of Christ-like cellular networks (others) is the organic "building block" for the life processes of his church. Our design orientation therefore necessarily starts on the inside with *you*—your redeemed, set-apart, gifted, Spirit-infused, kingdom-code-carrying self.

God, who imagined all living things uniquely, is more than simply the Maker of the universe; He is also its Designer. He does not just bring everything into existence; He crafts, formats, arranges, plans, frames, and interconnects everything He makes. By making and taking the precious material of human personhood and refining it through the experience of life, the Master Artisan forms each person into a precious one-of-a-kind work of art. We are formed by Him and created in His likeness, and not in the likeness of any other one person. His creative Holy Spirit lives in His people, allowing them to share in His exquisite creativity. This suggests that you are all at once a magnificent work of art *and* a gifted artist. We begin here not only because you are valuable to God but also because we believe emphatically that life is meant to be designed in accordance with the patterns of its Creator.

As you wrestle with this chapter, we want you, our readers, to acknowledge and love yourselves—to make some honest observations about your identity, how you are wired, and how your path has informed your life. As the book proceeds, we want you to have already wrestled with who you are, where you are, and how you are. We want ministry to flow out of the unique *you* that God loves, and we want you to like the life you are living.

Life by Design

A group of surfers in northern California are planting a church in a surf community while a gang of Christian bikers nearby are reclaiming the streets of a crime-ridden neighborhood. A proud Arizona cowboy-miner pastors a church full of people just like him. A painter and ceramic mold maker ministers in an arts community. A generational restaurant family holds night church in restaurants for the people who work there. Former substance abusers, now addicted to Jesus, have catalyzed a church planting movement by evangelizing, discipling, and raising leaders up from among those who have left their former cultures. Ministering in the name of Christ, they are all perfectly themselves.

Thomas Merton said, "The beginning of love is to let those we love be perfectly themselves, and not to twist them to fit our own image. Otherwise we love only the reflection of ourselves we find in them."[3] The problem, however, is not so much that we attempt to recreate people in our own image (though we do). The real issue in ministry is that we attempt to recreate both ourselves and others into the image of certain heroes that our church cultures admire and respect. We aim to reproduce Ricks, Bills, Neils, and Tims, and even Teresas—but never well enough. Our attempts, meanwhile, have helped us become experts at living unauthentic lives. How did we end up here?

Some ways of starting, leading, and growing churches, as well as all kinds of other organizations, have produced complex sets of management tools, processes, training programs, and coaching systems that help leaders know exactly what to do, and when and how to do it. When leaders wake up in the morning, there is a list of things they need to accomplish that day in order to stay focused on particular projects. They know how to hire, fire, coordinate, and evaluate. The successful leader in these paradigms knows how to structure work, and maybe even the whole of life. Ministry seems intentional and productive, which, after all, is a good thing, and these leaders are good people. We applaud those who can make this set of tools work for them and for their churches.

There are many, however, for whom this way of living and working never quite works. They live with a gnawing sense of dis-ease: something outside of themselves has infected their way of life, but there doesn't seem to be a way out. Someone, maybe even God, has created a productivity spreadsheet and is keeping record of how they rate in worship attendance, resident member-ship, and baptisms. Are these management tools the only way to prove one's ministerial adequacy? Do we have to take on someone else's model for life and ministry?

Dozens and dozens of people we know are no longer willing to live with the guilt that comes from just not living someone else's life well enough. They want their life back—their whole life. Still, many are afraid that the journey will lead them down a path of inef-fectiveness. It's a double bind. They want out, but as products of the American work ethic they are not certain about a way of living intentionally that will help them regain their life, retain their fruit-fulness, and sustain their future.

Linda still remembers the stunning moment when she first heard of the mathematical concept of the integer. An integer, of course, is a whole number, a complete unit with no fractions (fractures). It is the root word of *integrated* and *integrity,* which are core concepts in design. This was the concept she didn't have a name for but had already spent years trying to uncover. She remembers feeling, even in elementary school, a pressing need to be the same person on the inside as on the outside—a whole number. Discovering the concept, however, was only a first step. It was not until her rebirth in Christ many years later that she realized perfect integration or wholeness was a direction and not a destination on this side of eternity.

How about you? Are you learning to live life wholly? Are you experiencing the integrity of working and living in a way that makes sense in relationship to how you have been uniquely created . . . or are you chasing someone else's life? Have you embraced a way of living that nourishes you, your family and your community? Is it within your reach, or does mixing ministry with a life that is integrated and whole seem like an impossible dream?

An Artist's Tools

When adults choose their wardrobe, most do not simply base their decisions on what everyone else is wearing. Body shape and size, hair color, skin tone, and age come into play. So do things like climate and the culture in which one lives, lifestyle, and budget. Personal style is integrated around all of these components. Likewise, there are a number of components to consider in designing a life of service to God. Writing from a design perspective, we use some of the principles and vocabulary of design. Structure, space, texture, style, and form are themes that inform us and help us to live in whole, integrated ways that also reflect our individuality.

Meaningful Content and Intentional Structure

When Linda and her husband, Eric, host events in their home, guests sometimes bring them simple bunches of store-bought flowers. Delighted, Eric runs to the backyard and cuts a variety of greenery that he uses to build a new bouquet. Then, one by one he places the flowers, displaying their varieties of texture, shapes, and colors. By the time he is finished, the creation is so stunning that the flower givers are utterly amazed at their gifts. Nobody ever says, "What a great greenery structure you made." Of course not; they comment on the beautiful flower bouquet. These very same flowers could have easily been plopped as-is into water, but they would not have seemed even a fraction as lovely.

In this bouquet story, the flowers act as a focal point, even though the blooms are best displayed when the artist uses other foliage to create something much more beautiful. Christ *is* the focal point for the Christian's life. Those who consciously choose to pattern their lives in the way of Jesus find that the content of their lives is exceptional. A disciple, then, is one who chooses to live a life that is disciplined around the words and example of Jesus. Disciples do not draw attention to themselves by the kind of life they lead; they draw attention to Christ.

In life, as well as in art, when there is something predictable and ordered, it follows that the less predictable stands out. When Jesus and His disciples stood watching people making their predictable temple offerings, one poor widow who gave an extraordinarily small offering that day broke the ritual. The story of the widow's mite lives on because she did what was unusual. She gave everything she had. In a seasonally predicable night sky, one star shone in a singular way. Kings and shepherds alike followed it to a manger where a babe unlike any other was born.

Some people (maybe even you) recoil involuntarily at words like *predictability* and *structure*. But the seasoned creative knows that these concepts are wonderful and necessary components of any good design. Years of experience have taught us both that it can be a mistake to completely abandon structure such as Christian practices or disciplines or accountability relationships. Without these, well-intentioned even passionate leaders sometimes flounder.

Three interrelated concepts help create appropriate structure: practices, time, and relationships. Commitment to regular financial giving, for example, is a practice that flows out of a thankful, trusting relationship to God. The faithful prayer warrior sets the alarm on her cell phone to remember to pray for her missionary friends, or to call her prayer partner every day. The family eats together, glad that the table represents a predictable alignment at the end of the day (or the beginning of the day, according to family schedules). By design, God plans this kind of cadence and rhythm for our lives. He created the light and then separated it from the darkness. He gives us the structures of day and night, work and rest. He also gives us Sabbath. It is so important that not only humans but also animals, and even the land, are recipients of God's Sabbath rest (Exod. 23:12, Lev. 25:2–4). We are free to break cadence, but God is very clear: "Remember the Sabbath by keeping it holy."[4]

Jack Roberts, a mentor of many Christian leaders in the East Bay region of northern California, and his wife, Becky, are not Jewish, but they practice the rhythm of Sabbath by observing Shabbat in their home. Their sons, daughters-in-law, and an assortment of friends gather on Friday evenings around the same ritual. They light a candle, bless a loaf of fresh bread and sprinkle salt on it, pronounce the *shemah,* and thank the King of the Universe in both Hebrew and English. They eat together and they share stories about their busy week. As much as anything else Jack does to mentor leaders, an invitation to share Shabbat with his family helps to form them.

There are ways of practicing ministry and ways of designing a life of service to God that ignore the rhythms God put in place. We both know this because we are sometimes guilty of these very things and have experienced firsthand the discord of the nonharmonious lifestyle. Are you ever guilty of this same thing?

Interacting with White Space

Another lifestyle choice relates to what artists call white space. A critical aspect of design, the value of white space lies in its ability to create contrast. In a single letterform, for example, letters are defined not only by lines but also by the space in between the lines and the counterbalance of dark and light. When a piece of art is overly busy, it loses its ability to communicate anything other than noise. When all of our space and time is occupied, there is no way for its shapes and rhythms to be clearly seen.

Singapore is already a recognized world leader in education, but recently it has received international attention for redesigning learning in its public schools for the twenty-first century. Tharman Shanmugaratnam, the minister for education, specifically called for "creation of white space through content reduction." He said to Parliament, "[we] will seek to cut back on quantity . . . so as to provide more 'white space' in the curriculum, space which gives schools and teachers the room to introduce their own programmes, to inject more quality in teaching, or give students themselves the room to exercise initiative and shape more of their own learning."[5]

The familiar story of the Good Samaritan is about a man who understood the value of white space. The Samaritan had the time to stop his life to help a traveler in need, even though he was a busy man. His finances also allowed a little extra, so he chose to pay the innkeeper to care for the wounded man while he moved on with his life. Linda shared this perspective of the story with Paul Moxon, a church planter she mentors. Paul decided to implement what he calls a "Samaritan day" in his life. One day a week he leaves his schedule open and creates space for doing good and caring for people. This predictable island of time each week not only leaves Paul more able to absorb the unpredictable aspects of church starting but allows him to fulfill his preferred role of pastor/shepherd during a period in the life of the new church when administrative details swallow up much of his time. Using the tool of white space, he has found a way of structuring life so that he is better able to love himself and love others at the same time.

Not all people require the same amount of white space in their lives. Some of us require more or less sleep, are either energized or drained by being around crowds, and have large families, small families, or no family—all requiring differing amounts of time and attention. In some places in the world, everyday life takes more time to manage. Standing in line to pay a utility bill in Mexico City, waiting for public transportation in New York, dealing with power outages in Delhi, or looking for a parking space in San Francisco all burn up time; there is no way around it.

Rural life can also be crowded—driving on bad roads, pumping well water, or even having to always fix meals because of the absence of easily accessible family restaurants. The amount of time that it is reasonable to spend designing, refining, or re-aligning ranges vastly, depending on the situation. Some paintings look busy, and the white space isn't even noticed. Even in busy pieces of art, it is still the white space that gives it definition, and the same is true in the artwork of the self. Some ways of dreaming, hoping, and working are not compatible with reality, so it's important to give yourself permission just to stop. How much white space does it take for you to live honorably, obediently, and well? What does your white space look like? How does your ministry reflect and respect how God has wired humanity in general, and in you specifically? Is Sabbath keeping your normative practice, or is it one of the Big Ten with which you live more comfortably by disobeying?

Finding Your Style

Norman Rockwell and Andy Warhol were both populist artists who had something to say about American values. Nobody who even once viewed their works would ever confuse one with the other. Warhol adopted American icons, be it a simple Campbell's Soup can or a celebrity such as Marilyn Monroe. He played with the icon as a graphic image for the sake of the medium rather than for what it was. He took things that had value and almost stripped them, using angst and despair to protest the worldview that life is like a machine. Rockwell, on the other hand, was a sentimentalist. His style was pure Americana with a heart. He was down-home rather than urban, the complete opposite of Warhol. Always a populist, Rockwell took on themes of highly emotional public value and made them sentimental. Yet both artists have become American favorites.

You may not be a fan of either Rockwell or Warhol, but like them you have the capacity to discover your own style. In relationship to this chapter, this means that as a result of the integration of concepts, experiences, and practices you make intentional choices about a way of life that is whole, and good for you, others, and the planet. It isn't a difficult pursuit, though it needs wholehearted attention. There are literally thousands of good ways for Jesus' people to live and work.

In the mid-1990s, a few ethnically and culturally diverse San Francisco friends began planning a new church. Their lifestyles as San Franciscans and as "third culture" people, whose backgrounds reflected at least two other ethnicities, were also diverse. As they discussed the new church, they discovered that every one of them

yearned for a multicultural, multiethnic, multieverything community. Each had carried this dream for years, ultimately fueled
by faith that there will be a day when every knee bows and every
tongue confesses that Jesus is Lord.[6] Any earthly manifestation
of this promise seemed intensely beautiful, and the friends were
gratified by the opportunity to work toward their vision. Genuinely
missional people, schooled in the model of homogeneous church
growth, were skeptical. "You're planting a church for yourself,"
someone said to core team members. *Precisely.* The church planting
team individually and collectively acknowledged the life-forming
experiences, relationships, and realities that helped fashion their
identity and inform their way of life. As a result, they planted a
multicultural church that they loved and about which they were
passionate.

Style and Time Frame

Time frame is also part of style. People are oriented differently
around how they most naturally think about time, especially when
engaged in making plans and setting goals. Some people think in
the present and find it natural to think about decisions that influence the here and now. Others are future-oriented, even to the
point of finding it difficult to focus on present-day issues unless
they know how to connect them to the future. The Highlands
Ability Battery, an excellent tool for better understanding oneself,
groups people into three time-frame orientations: short-, medium-,
and long-range. People with short-range time frames like to know
how they can have an impact on the here and now. Those who are
aware of this aspect of themselves know how to engage in short-
term and project-oriented tasks that offer the potential for closure
and immediate gratification. Natural strategists, including people
with gifts of an apostolic type, have long-range time preferences.
They can work more easily than most without immediate rewards,
if they believe this helps achieve greater future rewards. Finishing short-term tasks is more challenging for these future-oriented
people, as is managing long-term relationships.

In our paradigm, this concept of time frame orientation has
some parallels, but it does not completely overlap with the question
of whether a person is more called to design, refine, or re-align.

Designers are frequently initiators who enjoy the beginning phases of a project but lack the interest and the skills to remain relationally connected and passionately involved over time. Refiners, and to some extent re-aligners, have a taste and respect for the past and are better equipped for the task of connecting the past to the future. They live well in present roles such as shepherd or teacher, although they may be quite visionary and forward-thinking. In what time frame do you most naturally live? What is an example of where you have used your best time frame? When has it been a struggle? How do these experiences affect your roles?

Appreciating Texture

The organic texture of a living thing is complex, infinitely deep, and always changing. An artificial plant may fool you, but on examination its textures betray it while the textures of nature are engaging and enduring.

Human life is also experienced as texture. There are rough places and smooth, tough abrasive relationships and relationships of relative ease, times that are regular and times that can be frighteningly irregular. The words *text, texture,* and *textile* all originate from the Latin root *textere,* which means "to weave." Our life stories are a kind of weaving too. Multiple threads of influence affect the strands of our lives. Factors often outside our control come together to color a fabric that is then lovelier and more complex. Regardless of the nature of the apostle Paul's thorn, the texture of his story heals and encourages: "My grace is sufficient for thee: for my strength is made perfect in weakness . . . for when I am weak, then am I strong."[7]

Japan, internationally recognized as a design culture, effectively incorporates both texture and its related concept of pattern into everyday life. Ancient gardens in Kyoto are replete with myriad patterns and textures: walkways, doorways, gates, and walls. Even in urban Japan, thoughtful design is reflected in manhole covers and the textures of pavement. These communicate messages as speed bumps do on American roads, but with a greater, aesthetically pleasing civility and grace.

This ability to communicate through pattern and texture is underappreciated in modern Western culture. Sameness and mechanical efficiency replace good texture in our living spaces and in our lives. With a little intentionality, however, it is possible to rise above slavish functionality and create textures that make life lovelier. Recently the Bergquists' friend Mark Scandrette organized an open mic time at the community center Eric directs. Professionals and street artists alike gathered to share stories, poems, and songs around the theme of hope. It was raw, spontaneous, and beautiful. Everyone contributed, many out of their pain and humiliation, and everyone was affirmed. In contrast, many of us hide our lives and the texture a life can communicate. It is chilling that our airbrushed lives, with their many hidden blemishes, carry more of the appearance of texture than they do the real deal.

Our friend Dieter Zander is a gifted pastor, musician, worship leader, and church starter. Early in life he was mentored by gifted Christian leaders, served on the staff of one of America's most notable churches, wrote a book, and married into a wonderful family. Last year, however, although relatively young and in excellent health, Dieter suffered a massive stroke. Utterly dependent, he had to relearn everything: language, walking, moving his gifted fingers, all of it. Through it all, he rose to the challenge, humbling and inspiring his community in new ways. He chose to live openly and honestly as he struggled with limitations. He visited friends with whom he could not verbally communicate, and he even played the keyboard in church services with the one hand that functioned better than the other. Meanwhile, his expressive eyes have not stopped dancing as he works untiringly toward healing and recovery. His life, which had once appeared fairly smooth textured, became exceedingly rough—but never more beautiful. Then again, John Milton was blind when he wrote *Paradise Lost*; Beethoven was deaf and never heard his Ninth Symphony outside of his own mind; and the Apostle Paul lived with some thorn that brought texture to his life.

Brennan Manning said, "To live by grace means to acknowledge my whole life story, the light side and the dark. In admitting my shadow side I learn who I am and what God's grace means."[8] Through the ages, God has spoken through Moses' stutter and the Apostle Paul's thorn in the flesh. What texture has God added to your life, and how can you embrace it so that that it forms and transforms you uniquely for His glory?

Form and Shape

Benjamin Franklin said it well: "There are three things extremely hard: steel, a diamond, and to know one's self." Knowing oneself, however, is more than knowing one's life purpose, mission, or calling. We are shaped for amazement, beauty, creativity, play, and relationship. James Thurber reminds us not to oversimplify or categorize one another: "I loathe the expression 'What makes him tick.' It is the American mind, looking for simple and singular solution that uses the foolish expression. A person not only ticks, he also chimes and strikes the hour, falls and breaks and has to be put together again, and sometimes stops like an electric clock in a thunderstorm."[9]

God clearly wired us all in such a way that we enjoy and do better at some things than other things. When we understand what our strongest God-given talents and abilities are, we learn to work in ways that are complementary, rather than contradictory, to them. Sometimes people confuse concepts such as natural ability with spiritual gifts or intelligence, but they are different things. By natural ability, we mean the inherited talents that are a part of who we are from the time they are formed in us. These abilities can be specific—such as a knack for public debate or grasping complex mathematical concepts—or generalized, such as relating well to all kinds of people.

We can express these abilities and strengths differently. For example, one artist may need to focus her whole life on the arts, while another may choose the arts as an extracurricular activity. In either case, the work each does is motivated by natural creativity, which seeks expression in whatever vocation the individual chooses. Some people shine at many things just because by personality they are committed, driven, or intelligent; but if the things they spend time doing are not in line with their natural abilities, those things just don't bring them as much joy over a long period of time.

In ministry, we sometimes adopt prescribed roles or scripts because they are "working" well, and seemingly bearing much fruit for others. We attend conferences where mega-fruit bearers challenge us in new ways, and sometimes our egos are challenged as a result. We want to bear much fruit too; after all, the mission of God is what we structure our lives around. So we stop working in ways that reflect how we are naturally and supernaturally created, change the way we do ministry, attempt to reengineer our personhood, and sometimes actually become more successful as a result. For a period of time this satisfies, but eventually we burn out and wonder why. It's because we are working contrary to how we are designed. It is also because we confuse fruit bearing with producing visible, countable results, as indicated by the common questions "How'd ya do last Sunday?" "How many showed up on Easter?" "Baptize anyone yet this year?"

The "E-Myth" is an idea behind a book series that addresses this phenomenon of being promoted out of one's gifts. In the business world, there is often an assumption that because an individual is an expert in some skill area, the next logical step is to start and manage the business side of work. This often-fatal assumption has implications for business models of ministry as well. The effective preacher, counselor, or mentor is not necessarily savvy or competent in relationship to the set of skills involved in leading a more organizationally complex church.

We learned this many years ago from experiences in dealing with marginalized communities. In proposing a deaf-language church, rather than just a deaf ministry of a hearing church, we envisioned a community where each member could lead and use his or her spiritual gifts. The difficulty we encountered was that in those days schools for hearing-impaired people did not help to equip students as leaders. The job of pastoral leadership was perceived as being too difficult. The same was true of Cambodian refugees from the same era. The Khmer Rouge had assassinated such a large number of the educated, wealthy, culturally connected people in the country that a virtually leaderless culture emerged. In both cases, the task of pastor/leader needed to be reduced to its level of greatest integrity (in math it is called the least common denominator): egalitarian relational and spiritual leadership, which turned out to be the only kind of leadership they needed so as to be a church after all. Darith Hay was a poor man who was good at only one thing: serving the needs of others. He turned out to be an outstanding pastor among new Cambodian refugees in Fort Worth, and later in San Diego.

A good example of reconciling one's gifts with one's goals or sense of calling and where one should be is shown by a seminary graduate we know who was interested in planting a church. At that time, most prospective planters considered only one paradigm: a "purpose-driven" model, requiring an entrepreneurial leader with excellent communication skills. Byron, however, was an introverted, timid leader who did not have great verbal skills. In spite of this, he was convinced that he was called to be a lead planter in a church plant. Allan asked him to engage in a one-year internship that would prepare him for the next chapter of his life. During the mentoring process, Byron discovered he had a passion and a talent for communicating through writing. He also realized he was a good listener and enjoyed helping people work through their problems. After the internship ended, Focus on the Family hired him to correspond with people writing to the organization for counsel. Byron enjoyed this work so much that he took additional course work, earned a counseling degree, and found a ministry that was more suited to how God had wired him.

How Are You Shaped?

Peter Drucker once said, "Most people think they know what they are good at. They are usually wrong."[10] He is pointing out that sometimes people imagine they are better at more things than they really are. We live in a day when there are so many "tools that fool": fonts that make us think our logos look good, multimegapixel digital cameras that make us think we are photographers, and Web design tools that make us believe we are excellent Web-site designers. Are we ever creative (at least in our own mind)!

In real life, though, not many people are good at more than a few things. William Herschel was an exception, an astronomer's astronomer. Most experts in his field have been great observers, great theorists, or great telescope makers, but Herschel was one of the few people who ever lived who had superior skills in all three areas. Church work is so demanding that sometimes leader roles seem to demand this kind of unusual, multifaceted proficiency that is historically equated with genius. Pastors have been taught to lead in a "*sola pastora*"[11] way. Sometimes we are fooled into believing we are actually that good. So it is important to ask: what are you *really, really* good at, what are you passionate about, and what do you love to do? In his book, *Get a Life: It Really Is All*

About You,[12] Reggie McNeal suggests asking oneself the following questions: What makes your heart beat faster? What brings you energy? What captures your attention?[13]

The Need for Soul Care

The biblically grounded practice of self-care, or soul-care, is still a fairly new concept for evangelicals, one on which Christians are divided. In his voluminous work *Foundations for Soul Care,* Eric Johnson makes the case for a perspective that is legitimately grounded outside the self: "Inwardness is ultimately valid if it is theocentric, Bible-based, and dialogical."[14] Self-care is considered, then, in light of the acceptance of our own human limitations. Ministers must set parameters that help us learn to care for ourselves because we are *not* perfect, we have needs, and we do not have all of the answers all of the time. If we refuse to admit that we are vulnerable, then over time an artificial caricature of an authentic self overtakes the real deal, and ministers especially begin to really believe they are invulnerable.

Evangelical Lutherans wrote a document to ministry candidates about the high expectations it places on those who serve in the denomination. This excerpt demonstrates some of its commitment to a healthy view of self: "The ordained minister needs to be an example of self-care, as well as caring for others. The significant demands of time and effort within the office of ordained ministry can lead one to neglect proper nutrition, exercise, and time for recreation. The congregation, or whatever agency or institution the ordained minister serves, should respect the need for the ordained minister to have adequate time for self-care."[15]

Conclusions

As she was editing this chapter, Linda received a phone call from Dave Maturo, whom she was recruiting to move to San Francisco. "Have you ever read the book *The Shaping of Things to Come?*"[16] he asked. Dave explained that the ideas of the book matched the yearnings of his heart for a missional way of life in the context of a like-minded community. Dave is not irresponsible, but for him it almost didn't matter how God supplied home and food. He simply wanted to pursue the kingdom of God in ways that seemed less possible in the older suburban community where he lived alone with his dreams. He knew that what he needed most was to nurture a new way of life and ministry, and not merely to find a job. Dave's quest reminded Linda of something she read in the prologue of Hermann Hesse's *Demian*: "But every man is more than just himself; he also represents the unique, the very special and always significant and remarkable point at which the world's phenomena intersect, only once in this way and never again. That is why every man, as long as he lives and fulfills the will of nature, is wondrous, and worthy of consideration."[17]

Our prayer for our readers is not that they adopt our ideas or models. Although we naturally have theological and paradigm preferences, we are not at this moment advocating any of them. Our hope, rather, is that you will accept the freedom Christ offers, and move a few steps in the direction that he is leading you. Once again, how do themes such as structure, space, texture, style, and form help you become and do those things to which you are uniquely called? To what are you willing to commit in order to more fully live your own life?

3

CULTIVATING COMMUNITY

A single cell [is] the simplest living thing, however, living things cannot exist alone. They exist within the framework or network of other living things. When a cell reproduces, it passes on not only its genes, but its whole cellular network. It is not simply the DNA that reproduces. Genes only function within the context of a network.
—FRITJOF CAPRA[1]

FROM THE TIME THEY WERE LITTLE CHILDREN, Orville and Wilbur Wright lived in the same place, shared their toys, and talked about their dreams. In 1912, Wilbur wrote, "Nearly everything that was done in our lives has been the result of conversations, suggestions and discussion between us."[2] Their prolific diaries prove that it was the genius of their sustained collaboration, and not one moment of inspiration, that caused them to become America's "fathers of flight." The brothers shared rare, legendary community. They trusted each other with their successes, their failures, and literally even with their lives.

The Wrights were more than two individually gifted brothers; they were joined in heart and soul. Gifted in complementary ways, they were capable of more together than either was individually. Charles Spurgeon, a nineteenth-century British pastor, understood genius in the same way. He wrote: "Communion is strength; solitude is weakness. Alone, the fine old beech yields to the blast and lies prone on the meadow. In the forest, supporting each other, the trees laugh at the hurricane. The sheep of Jesus flock together. The social element is the genius of Christianity."[3]

We know now that no organism can live in isolation. Instead, it is characteristic of all living systems to provide not only for individuals but also for some kind of collective network. In fields as diverse as complexity theory, complex adaptive systems, biology, mathematics, organizational psychology, and cognitive sciences, experts are learning the same lessons about this amazingly networked planet and the life on it. Hungarian author Frigyes Karinthy published a short story in 1929 titled "Chain-Links" that has stimulated social theorists for decades. The thesis of the story was that in light of new capabilities in communications and travel, the world was shrinking. Karinthy believed that humans were increasingly connected and were only around five relational links away from one another. "Chain-Links" propelled research leading to the now-popular idea that each of us is no more than six relational "steps" away from every person on earth (six degrees of separation).[4]

One way we might have approached this chapter is to revisit all the identity-forming processes we examined in the previous chapter. We could ask that each participant of a ministry team be assessed. Then, on the basis of experiences, spiritual gift inventories, strength-finding processes, and personality profiles, each person would typically be assigned a task in line with the apparent needs of the church. This way of working, however, says nothing about the interaction between the individuals who fulfill their assigned roles, according to their gifting and passions. In this structural model, teamship is assumed but may never be realized, mainly because structural assignments are often made presuming the church is an organization, rather than a true team. Studies prove that this way of organizing does not tend to produce the same quality of work or the same level of satisfaction as a group of people who negotiate real networks, meaning teams who recognize the group as an extension of the concepts of self discussed in the previous chapter. Breakthrough ways of thinking, designing, and producing happen best when people recognize the genius of connecting with one another. We know of several churches and networks that are now thinking of the leadership structure as a connected team rather than a hierarchical organization.

There is another word, besides "network" or "organization," for what we are talking about: *community,* a concept that these days seems a bit shopworn, threadbare, and misconstrued. So many things are termed *community* that the word carries little real meaning anymore. We talk about global community, local community, the workplace community, the arts community, and even the virtual community. Churches start small groups to encourage their parishioners to "do community together," and we run demographic profiles to discover the needs of our "target communities."

All of these usages of the word are valid in some contexts, but they are so overworked that most of us find our eyes glazing over at its mention, and the concept loses particular significance. Additionally, the historic individualism of Western culture neither values nor understands the sense of true community common in most non-Western cultures. This lack of understanding or experience of true community affects everything from friendships and local community expressions, likened unto the tribal campfires of old, to the relational capacity for Kingdom engagement. This means humans are yearning for more intimate connection to a group of people with a common passion and purpose for living and experiencing life together. A younger generation of Westerners now feel cheated. They react vigorously against individualism and yearn for community, but they lack the formative experiences and skills necessary to discover the essence of what they long for. This chapter is about choosing the genius of community. It is about conceptualizing biblical community as integral to the meaning and activity of the church (that is, biblical principles of community and mission), and considering how these principles factor into the overall design process. You will make all kinds of decisions about what community means to you, the degree to which you value it, and how it can be nurtured in healthy ways. These are inside-out design decisions about a church's long-range core capacity for both community and mission.

Two Spheres of Community

We propose that everyone can potentially experience true community in two spheres. First is "microcommunity," which includes the people nearest to us: family, intimate friends, mentors, teammates, and those with whom we share a close community of faith. These are the peoples God uses most frequently to shape us and teach us. They are who Wendell Berry called out when he wrote: "A community is the mental and spiritual condition of knowing that the place is shared, and that the people who share the place define and limit the possibilities of each other's lives. It is the knowledge that people have of each other, their concern for each other, their trust in each other, the freedom with which they come and go among themselves."[5] By using the term *microcommunity,* we aim to suggest the wealth and beauty of intimate relationship that is difficult to capture in words.

Nelson Mandela said it well in his autobiography by teaching us the word *ubuntu.* It's a Bantu word we should make our own. It is so rich that linguists call a "crowditude" of other words to the rescue to express its nuances. In academic terms ubuntu is "the quality inherent in the fact of being a person with other persons." When he uses it in his autobiography, Mandela translates it into English as "fellowship," literally camaraderie, or in context "fellow citizenship." In fact, ubuntu means much more, well beyond that: a way of being human, a way of conducting oneself as a human being, a practice of mutual humanity.[6]

Ubuntu entails not only some aspects of identity but also how one's identity is defined and formed in connection with others. Even in the business world, retailers have identified microcommunity as a critical issue: "There is already a great deal written about the importance of the customer in today's online world. But what of the customer's micro-community? Every individual has his or her own micro-community; a closely-knit circle of family, friends and key influencers."[7] Microcommunity or ubuntu, transformed and empowered by the Holy Spirit, intrinsically forms the next layer of life-giving DNA in our continued conversation about the church. We started with who we are (self) and now we are considering an extension of it: who life and mission are done *with,* that is, our microcommunity. Because it is held accountable to scripture, a new church is beautiful at birth, and it has the potential to mature in beauty if it abides by some deep sense of microcommunity. As designs happen, we challenge our readers to understand and aspire to live out this principle.

Macrocommunity

Just as all organisms are composed of a close cellular network, they also belong to larger, loosely connected networks. Systems biologists are now astounded by the degree of interdependency and self-organization they have discovered throughout nature. What used to be called a "food chain" of species domination is now seen as a vast cooperative web. In physics, the "butterfly effect" refers to a theory about the intricate interconnectivity of the planet: the flap of a butterfly's wings in one part of the world can bring about small changes in the atmosphere that potentially alter the path of a tornado or a tsunami somewhere else in the world. Each person and each microcommunity also interfaces in macrocommunity.

Macrocommunity can include a global community, an Internet community, a transnational work community, or any number of sets of extended relationships, even to the uttermost parts of the world. It can be argued scripturally that there is a macrocommunity of sorts that connects the church through generations. It can also be argued that there are healthy ways of talking about people's relationship to the earth's nonhuman populations that nurture human existence. In this chapter, though, when we use the term *macrocommunity* we *specifically refer to people who make up the "neighbor-sphere" of our everyday existence.* Neighbor-spheres are the people of the city or neighborhood in which we dwell who influence and inform how we live our lives. These are acquaintances, both secular and spiritual, who are not participants in our microcommunity of faith yet are integral to the conversation of design in this book and in our readers' lives. They influence our lives and our decisions, and we influence theirs. In microcommunity, people travel life's journey together, share many of the same values, and work toward such common causes as being a family, being a healthy church, transforming our macrocommunities, and pleasing God together.

Along the way, something Jesus-like may happen. At that point members of a neighbor-sphere may begin sharing a more potent microcommunity, even faith-centered communities. As we become adept at living in these two spheres, micro and macro, our lives take on a rhythm as unself-conscious as breathing in and breathing out. Practice in one sphere affects our ability to live more fully in the other, but disregarding or failing to take advantage of God's design to place us in meaningful communities of relationships (both micro and macro) can result in living an uninspired and isolated existence, never fully entering into what Christ intended for us, and failing to discover the incarnational lifestyle of Christ. Both of us are part of faith communities in different cities that experience microcommunity, and together we encourage one another to look beyond ourselves into the macrocommunity.

Virtual Community

Technological discovery brought about another evolution in the nature of macrocommunity: the virtual community. But do online social networks qualify as community or not? Some of our students say yes, they qualify. They cite online communities ranging from gaming groups to virtual churches. Other people say that online churches are not only impossible but also heretical. Yet for some, the online church is the only one they will ever know. A missionary told Allan a story of an Iranian woman who came to Christ with nothing but Internet access to inform her. The Internet makes the gospel accessible to people without Bibles; it also connects people in ways that redefine paradigms of community, microcommunity, and online neighbor-spheres.

In 1501 Aldine Press in Italy published a small-type, paperback pocket version of Virgil. It made the classic poems available to a large number of people. Next they began publishing fiction, an act that radically altered the potential of the average person to become a reader.[8] Aldus Manutius, the publisher, not only embraced the reality that the printing press was here to stay but started to imagine how the world could be different as a result. In a similar way, the Internet is here to stay, and so are virtual communities. People are already finding religions, being converted to various forms of faith, and meeting as communities of belief in these virtual communities, whether or not the church agrees. The first year after the popular social network site Meetup.com began, the fifteen most active groups included witches, vampires, atheists, pagans, and ex-Jehovah's Witnesses.[9]

Some people use their computers like typewriters that also do e-mail, without taking advantage of the machine's huge capacity.

In the same way, most churches know about, and many have developed, websites and a few blogs (writing public online journals), while fewer produce podcasts or videocasts (online audio or video files). A generation ago, the perception was that a church was viable if it had a building. Today, a church is perceived as viable if it has a website. Although most churches still conceptualize their sites simply as places where people come to find information about the church, so much more is possible. What would you do with technology if you could? What kinds of biblical community do you believe can be formed online, and how can online community enhance your church's ministry?

Discovering Microcommunity

The Henri Nouwen Society Website shares its vision for helping to create and nurture community: "Christian community happens whenever we gather as God's beloved—whether at home, work, or church—to embrace our vulnerability and discover our strengths. It happens when we enter solitude with God and find others in God. It happens when we reach inward to our wounded hearts with acceptance and outward to a wounded world with compassion and creativity."[10]

We agree, adding that for followers of Christ microcommunity is of course shared with at least one other human, but also with the Spirit of God, who is present and sharing in our spiritual union. The trite saying that "the family that prays together stays together" is actually a weighty spiritual truth because the biblical understanding of community is rooted in the capacity for common prayer. In Luke 10, when Jesus sent out seventy disciples to be missionaries, He gave them specific instructions. Though the story is brimming with missiological principles, it begins with the mandate to pray together in pairs. Jesus told the thirty-five teams to imagine the potential of the Kingdom with God's eyes, and He told them to pray together, asking the Father to send more laborers into the field (Luke 10:2). This was more than something Jesus commanded the disciples to do; it was a prayer that is in the heart of God to answer. The petitions of a microcommunity gathered in His name empowers those praying to see the world with God's perspective.

The Luke 10:2b prayer movement[11] started in Denver in 2002 when two men began praying together daily that God would send missionaries and church planters to the harvest fields where they lived. Many people in a number of cities and states joined the men in this prayer. Over time, the men who initiated the movement experienced something that extended far beyond God's miraculous provision of workers for the harvest. It seemed clear that as a result of gathering around prayer, people began to grow tremendously in their relationship with each other and with God. Regardless of their initial level of spiritual maturity, those who participated in these enlivened microcommunities started to naturally incorporate scripture into their prayers and reported a sustained intimate communion with Father, Son, and Spirit.

Types of Microcommunity

Family

When the apostle Paul used a metaphor to refer to the union among God the Father, Christ the Son, and the Christian who is adopted into the divine family, he used familial words. We are invited to call out Abba: "Because you are sons, God sent the Spirit of his Son into our hearts, the Spirit who calls out, 'Abba, Father'" (Gal. 4:6). We are members of God's household (Eph. 2:19). The wholesome nuclear family is God's ideal. Those who are blessed with loving spouses, parents, siblings, children, and grandchildren inherit the DNA of microcommunity quite naturally. Both of us enjoy the amazing gift of our spouses playing primary roles in our microcommunities. It is an indescribable joy to know a parent-child relationship that is intimate enough to pray together, talk about the truths of the Kingdom, and experience it firsthand through living life together. This kind of family becomes salt and light, to the macrocommunity and to others in their immediate microcommunities as well.

Unfortunately, realities such as divorce, distance, and death make the experience of healthy family relationships increasingly rare. Even healthy families are influenced by a worldview that has often caused us to compartmentalize work, church, and home relationships in a way that makes it even more difficult to find and pass on valuable relational principles and practices. But we are wired as humans to be connected, and many people who have never experienced this now seek it for themselves. Sometimes the quest means that unrelated people begin to think of themselves as family. For example, a number of young adults relate to Allan and his wife, Kathy, as adopted children, even though they have their own families. They include several new refugee teens for whom the Karrs serve as legal guardians. This does not diminish the love of these adopted young people for their own families. It merely highlights a craving for the kind of love that people with a shared mission can discover in the context of unity with Christ.

How about you? Could it be valuable for you to move past the modern separation of work, play, school, and family time? Do you yearn for a way of life that places intimate family relationships in the center of other microcommunity relationships? Are you open to defining your family by the relationships beyond by spiritual and relational, rather than mere biological, DNA? Who else does your family include? You and your family, intentionally or not, model something about the household of God. How will you factor family into your church design?

Mentors

About three years ago, some of Allan's closest friends were engaged in a running conversation. They observed that they loved God very much and had served him most of their lives, most of them in some kind of ministry, and mostly in vocational roles in the church. They admitted that even though they saw glimpses of God's power in their lives and ministries, if they were transparently honest they really weren't experiencing anything that resembled the power of the Holy Spirit. They genuinely desired that the Kingdom of God be more evident in their everyday lives. They longed to serve God in such a way that the events of their days could be explained only by the work of God's Spirit in them.

Allan says they became sickeningly aware that thus far they had been relying more than they realized on their own intellect, creativity, work ethic, and education for their success. All of these things are gifts from God, but they were trusting more in these attributes than in a vibrant union with Christ. They finally realized that they needed a different approach for coping and dealing with life and ministry. From this discussion, they began to look into the life of Jesus and learn an old practice of His—mentoring—and imagine what that would look like in this day and age, and how it could bridge across cultures. The strategy they followed for years resulted in some good things, but nothing that resembled the potential God wanted to release in their lives.

Mentoring is another way to release the power of God in micro-community. Mentors spend time with fewer people in more intense interactions but have a potentially greater impact on their lives. Mentoring includes spending time together, praying together, discussing life's issues together, and supporting one another in hard times. It includes modeling of character and courage, and handling disappointment with grace. It means encouraging, challenging, and holding mentees accountable to their God-given potential. This was also a key component of Jesus' ministry. By design He had twelve disciples (eleven that got it), but there were three with whom He spent most of His time. Jesus also gave His time to a small group of women (two Marys and Martha). Who are the people into whom you are pouring your life? Have you asked God to show you how to invest your relational time and energy? To what extent does communion with the Spirit influence how you spend time with others?

Teams

Larry and Carol Oftedahl were founding members of Pathways Community Church in Santee, California. After a few years, Carol became an administrative assistant and treasurer for Pathways, working with pastor Phil Herrington. When Larry was diagnosed with Lou Gehrig's disease, it seemed like a short time until he became completely disabled. He could not feed or groom himself, or even move from his bed to his wheelchair and back. Pastor Phil began visiting the Oftedahl home every evening to move Larry into bed. Other church leaders joined in. They helped get Larry out of bed in the mornings and took him to men's meetings or whatever else Larry wanted to do. Some accompanied him around the neighborhood, where Larry collected recyclables for the purposes of making money he could donate to the church he loved. The associate pastor, Ross Shepherd, took him to ball games. Larry often accompanied Carol to work, where he became a regular part of the office scene. Larry died a few years later, a beloved member of the Pathways team (where Carol still works).

Larry's life was both enriched and enriching to the end because he was a member of a microcommunity where Christ was the center and where members and pastors acted together as teams to do God's work. We suggest that teams are microcommunities of practice that work together in ways that acknowledge their interdependency as well as their dependency on Christ. The microcommunity is more than the sum total of its members; it is also about the group's interactions, identity, behaviors, and memories. This is what Scripture means by the functioning Body of Christ.

We ask teams that lead churches, as microcommunities of followers of Jesus, to consider how their spontaneous friendships, intimacy, shared passions, and interdependencies shape microcommunity and inform the design of an organization. The question is thus, "What are we called to do and become together?" We, the church, have sometimes forgotten that God wants His bride to be beautiful holistically, in mind, body, Spirit, and personality. Sometimes we focus on only one aspect of the church, such as its mission, and then are content to let relationships develop only in that context. A church culture begins to emerge where the fellowship of the microcommunity is only a byproduct of mission rather than something beautiful in its own right. In doing so, we are missing much of the richness and power God intended us to experience as we live out who we are in Christ. This concept of team as microcommunity permeates Scripture. The writer of Ecclesiastes says: "Two are better than one, because they have a good return for their work: If one falls down, his friend can help him up. But pity the man who falls and has no one to help him up! Also, if two lie down together, they will keep warm. But how can one keep warm alone? Though one may be overpowered, two can defend themselves. A cord of three strands is not quickly broken" (Eccl. 4:9–12).

In recent decades, and for many reasons, church leaders are beginning to explore team pastoring. Some, like Hirsch and Frost, call for a re-alignment around the APEST gifts.[12] This idea is taken from the leadership gifts listed in Ephesians 4:11, specifically the apostolic, prophetic, evangelistic, shepherding, and teaching gifts. New examination of the distribution of spiritual gifts in microcommunities is reminding the church that all of the pastoral gifts, passions, and skills do not need to be (and usually cannot be) manifested in the person of a single lead pastor. In addition, there are vital conversations regarding the difference between the office of the pastorate and the biblical role of the pastor in the body of Christ. Some approach this conversation from the viewpoint that "pastor" is an office of an institution or denomination, properly trained, appointed, ordained, and elected. Others acknowledge the biblical role of a pastor but propose that it is an authority given by God in the natural maturation of a church, such that a leader of character and wisdom naturally emerges.

Several questions need to be considered at this point. Do you value the ideas of microcommunity and yearn to be a part of a team? If not, why not? What holds you back? Are you interested in a model where several people in the team can exercise the biblical roles of leadership? If not, what is your rationale? Are you willing to be vulnerable in your leadership style and flexible in defining roles according to the gifts of those in your microcommunity? Are you willing for your organization and programs to be developed around these values?

Church

We live in an era of church history where there is considerable tension over a working definition of *church*. Most people try to understand it in a way that faithfully reflects what they personally believe the Bible says. Many also factor in their various church traditions. Different streams of Christian faith, and even individuals within those traditions, simply define the word in their own way. We two are from a "*sola scriptura*" church background and thus attempt a definition as free as possible from any model, or even from being based in a particular culture. For several years, Allan has been using the general definition of *church*: The church is a group of transformed followers of Jesus, who perceive themselves to be the Body of Christ in their local community and to the nations, and live as such.

The perception by the church that they are the church is a significant distinction between a Bible study and a small group.[13] For example people often ask what the difference is between a house church and a home Bible study. The answer is one group perceives and believes itself to be a church, and the other group doesn't. This affects not only their identity but the scope of their mission and ministry responsibility toward their macrocommunity, including how the microcommunity matures and grows together as they decide to be the church and what that will look like, as it is intentional about transforming the macrocommunity, partnering with all segments of society who care about the same thing Jesus cares about.

Occasionally, Allan begins a class discussion by asking his class to define *church*. Almost every time, early in the conversation, someone responds, "Where two or three come together in my name, there am I with them" (Matt. 18:20). The student is certain he or she has articulated a particularly edgy thought. Allan disagrees, much to the student's surprise, though for an unanticipated reason. Most students think the edgy part of their response is the "two or three" in the quote. Actually, an excellent biblical case can be made that the body of Christ can indeed be alive and well in a community with just a few people. The issue with the passage quoted in Matthew 18:20 defining the church is not that "two or three" is too small to be a church but the fact that it reflects a core ecclesiological misunderstanding of the nature of the church. It is not only the church when it is gathered. We are the church all the time—gathered together or not, big or small.

Size is not the determinant of what makes a church, yet some institutions have a predetermined size built into their policies. In spite of this, many cities, villages, and jungles all over the world have only a few followers of Jesus, sometimes numbering in single digits, and as a group they identify as a church and form a vital microcommunity of faith, even if structurally it is informal. When thinking of microcommunity in the context of church, we affirm that even small numbers of people can function as a church, and sometimes larger models of church miss out on the microcultural benefits. Larger churches usually overcome this with an attempt to have intimacy in class settings, or small-group strategies.

Our current Christian culture defines *church* as the gathering of believers. Most people, when asked to share about their churches, inevitably describe some primary gathering—the name of the church, the location of the building, and the time of the services. If pressed for more, they talk about the content of a worship service, the style of music, the type of preaching, the variety of programs for children and youths—in other words, the gathering. Certainly, Scripture also commands gathering: "Let us consider how we may spur one another on toward love and good deeds. Let us not give up meeting together" (Heb. 10:24–25). If we were being quite literal about scripture, we might speak of daily gatherings, not just Sunday meetings. It is a problem that our church culture defines church as a gathering. Matthew 18:20 is not a complete definition of church, because taken alone it reinforces poor ecclesiology. In reality, the church is the Body of Christ 168 hours a week as it relates to the macrocommunity and microcommunity, not just the one to five hours per week when people gather together for public worship. As Tim Chester and Steve Timmis say, "People need to encounter the church as a network of relationships rather than a meeting you attend or a place you enter. Mission must involve not only contact between unbelievers and individual Christians, but between unbelievers and the Christian community."[14]

It is clear from studying the commands of Scripture, especially the commands of Jesus, that some apply to gathering, but most of the commands of Jesus cannot be followed except by living them out in the context of life. Luke 10:25–37 is an account of a Jewish lawyer asking Jesus how to inherit eternal life. In the conversation that follows, the Lord articulates what has come to be called the Great Commandments. "Love the Lord your God with all your heart and with all your soul and with all your strength and with all your mind and, 'Love your neighbor as yourself'" (Luke 10:27). Some have adopted that verse to define public worship as a purpose of the church. But this verse actually implies a life that reflects our love of God twenty-four/seven, not just an hour or two a week when the church sings and prays together. If it is intentional that the command means to love God all the time, then logically to fulfill most of this commandment we have to leave the gathering to obey the majority of it. In the past, some have pointed out in dialogue that we typically spend one-fourth to one-third of every day sleeping. They insist that surely I wasn't trying to imply we are supposed to love God while we are sleeping. Besides revealing their confusion that following Jesus is more about doing than being, they live such foundational lives that they forget that even in the doing part of our faith we could be sleeping in the wrong bed, or with the wrong person, and that yes, you can honor or dishonor God even while sleeping. To follow most of this part of the Great Commandments, you have to leave the gathering and go live it—and live it in microcommunity with others.

A couple of years ago, Hugh Halter and Matt Smay spoke to Allan's class and talked about "engaging culture" and "developing community," a description of sound missiological principles. They pointed out that in international settings missionaries spent time learning the culture and making friends and later added structure. In a way, they were describing what we are calling macrocommunity and microcommunity. Through the years, we have observed many church leaders and church planters who have given structure to their church following the prescribed processes of their denomination, or on the basis of personal preferences or copies of "successful" models in other communities. We are suggesting that what our local church becomes in structure and model should come from an intersection of scriptural principles, a passionate understanding of who we personally are in Christ, understanding and love for our macrocommunity, and the distinctive characteristics and accountability of our microcommunity—and ultimately an expression of Jesus' principle of the Kingdom of God.

Emerging Community Issues

Of the many emerging themes surrounding the topic of community, we have selected two that we think will continue affecting the church most dramatically. They are generational differences in the understanding of microcommunity, and the changing role of women. Depending on your age and geography, these things are either already seriously significant or will be within the next decade.

Generational Differences

While Allan was in Istanbul recently, he became aware of a microcommunity issue that is a growing concern even in global contexts. The international workers he met there were grouped as work teams. For the older generation, "team" just meant a laboring together based on assigned tasks. However, the younger generation was more likely to enter their jobs with high expectations of what it meant to be part of a team. They left friends and family anticipating that when they arrived in a new land they would become part of new families—that is, of teams. When their expectations of sharing *communitas* were not realized, they felt frustrated and misled. The older generation was frustrated too. Undoubtedly, they had worked all their lives in institutions that used the same classic, functional approach to organizational design. They felt the younger generation's relational focus was, in many ways, just a waste of time. Some from an older generation, or even young people from an institutional value system, don't seem to understand or crave the camaraderie and accountability of a team. We think that generational issues surrounding the meaning of microcommunity will continue to plague not only churches, but culture at large for years to come.

The Changing Role of Women in Culture

Fifteen years ago, Linda dropped by the home of a church planter to talk about some business matter. When his wife greeted her, Linda commented on her new hairstyle. Then they resumed the church planting conversation. At some pause in the conversation, Linda again acknowledged the church planter's wife, commenting on how comfortable she had made their home. The church planter was puzzled: "I don't get it. First you're a church planter, then you're a woman, and then you're a church planter, and then you're a woman again. Which are you: a church planter or a woman?"

Linda is not a church planter despite being a woman; she is a church planter in the context of being a woman. The Father uniquely shaped her in His image: male and female He created them in the image of God (Gen. 1:26–28). Being a woman does not mean Linda loves Tupperware parties, but it does mean she has access to them. A few decades ago, while planting a church in a new subdivision, Linda had a difficult job penetrating her semiclosed community. One day, after surveying as much of the neighborhood as she could, she noticed a flyer posted on a community board inviting women to a Tupperware party. She decided to attend, purchased a few pieces, and at the end of the party was invited to three more parties. Everyone in her family received Tupperware for Christmas that year, but Linda also built relationships with many women, and eventually a church was birthed.

Now, Linda's work connects her with a number of Bay Area women who are using their church planting gifts for the sake of the Kingdom. Marian leads a team that teaches English and plants churches among Guatemalans. Elizabeth works with Marian but is starting a new group for young adults. Gail's focus is a children's ministry among Hispanics in an apartment community. Her goal is that it will become a new church. Elena's husband is the pastor of a new church, but Elena is clearly the strategist and outreach coordinator. Jennifer, who speaks Mandarin, is in the early stages of work among Mongolians. Esther is the founder of the Chinese Restaurant Ministry, which meets for worship, prayer, and Bible study in restaurants at 10:00 p.m., after the restaurants close, and this design is being used all over the country. Loren is active as a leader in a network of house churches. Each woman is in love with Jesus and passionately involved in the work of God's Church.

Allan is also committed to being creative in finding ways in which women who are gifted and passionate about their calling can serve God. He has tailored positions that that allow women a place of service in church planting. This in turn unleashes what they have to offer as missionaries, design catalysts, ethnographers, and social entrepreneurs.

Perhaps the next thing our readers anticipate our saying is that the church is changing, and therefore it is allowing women to take leadership roles. Maybe this is true, but the point we wish to make is that *women* are changing. Linda has been supported as a church planter by her own very conservative denomination for more than twenty-five years. She has mentored, led, and strategized, and she has been affirmed repeatedly for these activities. What's changed? Women are now learning to embrace the reality that God has a place for them after all, and if they rise to the challenge we will have double the number of people to do the work of the Kingdom of God.

4

PATTERNS THAT HONOR GOD

The miracles of the church seem to me to rest not so much upon faces or voices or healing power coming suddenly near to us from afar off, but upon our perceptions being made finer, so that for a moment our eyes can see and our ears can hear what is there about us always.
—WILLA CATHER[1]

HAVE YOU EVER WONDERED why so many of the most commonly used letters in our alphabet (a, e, r, s, t, d) are located on the left hand side of the keyboard where they must be typed with the left hand? Somewhere between 70 and 90 percent of the world's population is right handed, so people would type faster if they typed these letters with their right hand. Most of us never think about it. A more user-friendly keyboard was designed in 1936 by August Dvorak. Its use improves a typist's accuracy by 50 percent and increases speed by 20 percent. However, Christopher Shole's 1874 QWERTY keyboard, still in use today, helped those in his era type faster. Shole intentionally placed more commonly used keys on the left to slow down typists so that their speed would not cause the elevated keys of the early typewriter to jam. Slower, in this case, was faster. By the time Dvorak patented his new keyboard, the QWERTY keyboard was so widely in use that the world felt no need to make the shift. Shole's keyboard became a fact of life.

This awareness problem factors into many areas of life; the theology of the church is no exception. Stuart Murray addresses it in his book *Church Planting: Laying Foundations:*

> All church planters [and all evangelists] operate within theological frameworks, but often these are assumed rather than articulated and adopted uncritically rather than as the result of reflection. Theological principles may influence strategy and practice less than unexamined tradition or innovative methodology. . . . An inadequate theological basis will not necessarily hinder short-term growth, or result in widespread heresy among newly planted churches. But it will limit the long-term impact of church planting, and may result in dangerous distortions in the way in which the mission of the church is understood.[2]

In this chapter, we hope to help designers, refiners, and re-aligners understand their theological framework well enough to avoid dangerous distortions of the mission, and find their place as the beautiful bride of Christ.

Consequences of an Unarticulated Theology

Murray's proposal that "theology is more often assumed than articulated" holds true not only in the context of church plant-ing and evangelism but also in mission, ecclesiology, and almost every area of church life. The repercussions of having adopted the QWERTY keyboard are mostly speed and accuracy, but the conse-quences for churches that live with unarticulated theologies are more treacherous. The Society for the Advancement of Ecclesial Theology (SAET) is a network of pastor-scholars who have also recognized that theology seems be the work of the local church. In their online introductory letter to potential members, they comment:

> Unlike the early days of North American evangelicalism, our most significant theologians now reside almost exclusively in the acad-emy, too often disconnected from the press and weight of local church ministry. In an age that has rightly emphasized the rela-tionship between social location and theological formation, it is the belief of the SAET that the contemporary separation of praxis

from theological formation has resulted in the loss of a distinctly ecclesial voice in evangelical theology.[3]

One important reason we are focusing on theological patterns is that the best church designs are the ones that fuse axis and praxis—what we believe and what we choose to do about it.

Marriage of Church and Culture

Our failure to articulate our theology opens the door to an erosion of mission, and our churches can become quite different from what we intended. Culture feels no pressing need for a new keyboard design, but the church is beginning to realize that self-examination is critical, particularly at this point in history. The church has allowed itself to be shaped not only by theology but also by compromises with culture, politics, business, economics, and the entertainment world. Daniel Williams worries that "biblical exegesis is too often guided by no other authority than the marketplace of ideas and the social and emotional agenda of the congregation."[4] To make our point, here is a really wild story about a well-intentioned Georgia church that came up with an idea for an Easter outreach event.

> We decided if we were going to do it, we were going BIG, the pastor said. The church dropped 50,000 eggs into a park from a helicopter and twelve thousand people rushed the field. Immediately, they were knocked down and trampled. Parents pushed down children and grabbed their eggs. Hundreds of children were separated from their parents, crying, and left without eggs. Other parents screamed and many fell to the ground crying because they couldn't find their children. Three people had heart attacks and four passed out![5]

What was the resurrection message this church communicated to its community that day? All churches are susceptible to distortion; this particular church was just more energetic than most in trying to reach its community. The modern church is a product of its culture and has quite naturally contextualized its theology, forms, and practices to its own period of history. But now we are at the end of an era, waiting for the dawn of a new one. We should not be overly critical of one another. Almost every one of us has lived, taught, and preached in light of a faith that makes adaptations to our own culture and era. In some parts of the West, the fog seems to be thinning a bit faster than in others, but even the capacity to see through it seems to be based on the rate of change found in the places we live in the world as much as by our individual or collective wisdom. The "pioneer" voices among us are not necessarily smarter or wiser, or even more prophetic. Sometimes they simply live in places such as the San Francisco Bay Area, Seattle, New York, Austin, Bangalore, Sydney, and Dublin. Cities of this kind encourage curiosity and mobilize creativity. From them, ideas travel, making it easier to see the future. From such places the indicators say that our ship is far closer to the land before us than to the land we left behind. Missiologist George Hunsberger assures us, "All the clearest voices tell us that the *corpus Christianum,* the Constantinian arrangement, and the world of Christendom that guided our thinking about ourselves for 1,500 years, is not coming back."[6]

A Time for Change

Most of us know Willow Creek Church in Chicago as one of the most influential churches in North America. After modeling a new way of church for thousands of leaders for thirty years, they evaluated themselves though extensive research and discovered that they had made some monumental mistakes. For example, they discovered that the way Willow Creek approached programs created dependency on staff and other church leaders and was not producing disciples who knew how to help themselves become more mature Christians. They were surprised too that a higher level of participation in church programs did not necessarily lead to people becoming better followers of Christ. They openly acknowledged their mistakes, and Greg Hawkins, the executive pastor, summarized the church's position: "Our dream is that we fundamentally change the way we do church . . . that we take out a clean sheet of paper and we rethink all of our old assumptions, and replace it with new insights—insights that are informed by research and rooted in Scripture. Our dream is really to discover what God is doing and how he's asking us to transform this planet."[7]

Like Willow Creek, other congregations are beginning to acknowledge that even the transitions the church has made in the last several decades are not as helpful as they once were. The 2008 U.S. Religious Landscape Survey by the Pew Forum on Religion and Public Life, based on interviews with more than thirty-five thousand adults, found that the United States is on the verge of becoming a minority Protestant country. In addition, although 31 percent were raised Catholic, today just 24 percent are Catholic adherents. This is despite high Catholic immigration in recent years. Among those age eighteen to twenty-nine, one in four are not affiliated with any religion. We recognize and mourn the statistical evidence that Christianity is fast becoming a marginalized culture. Riddell, Kirkpatrick, and Pierson, all of whom are pursuing alternative types of worship experiences, say: "The Christian Church is dying in the West. This painful fact is the cause of a great deal of avoidance by the Christian community . . . it is not only possible for Christianity in the West to falter, it is apparent that the sickness is well advanced."[8]

Hauerwas and Willimon encourage us in what Bruggemann,[9] and later Frost,[10] called our situation of exile: "The church should be resident alien where we should anticipate that the concerns of the church and the concerns of the state are different."[11] Despite these theologians' assertion that "exile" is an invigorating place for the church to live, the body of Christ is nevertheless experiencing rampant separation anxiety as the values of church culture and the values of North American culture grow further apart.

Remembering the Paradigm Behind Us

We stand among a host of others who write on how the Enlightenment's social paradigms have crept into Christian traditions. Models of reality that are completely alien to earlier Christian eras have shaped both our theology and our practices. It is critical to consider, as objectively as possible, how the Enlightenment has affected our ecclesiology, our missiology, and ultimately our Christology. Of the numerous philosophies and concepts that intertwine in the Enlightenment, here we surface just a few that are most crucial to the design, refinement, and re-alignment issues of this chapter.

The World as a Collection of Things

First, in modernism *the world is seen as a collection of things that may be dominated, ordered, counted, and possessed by people.* This view of the world leads to an understanding of the universe that is mechanistic, deterministic, compartmentalized, and organized foundationally (hierarchically). More is better than less, and large is better than small. This is the world that invented mass production and franchises. It has also been the "era of the organization." Business and organizational theory, efficiency flow charts, and multinational corporations organize and manage people, things, and information in an increasingly global economy.

This aspect of modernity is not necessarily negative, but it is something that was culturally inherited, and not inherent to the nature of the church. It is not the existence of these ideas that is troublesome to our ecclesiology; it is that they are so readily embraced without questioning the extent to which they serve the meaning of the gospel and the mission of the church. Unwittingly we confuse entrepreneurial business leaders (people who control, count, order, and expand organizations) with apostolically gifted servants of God. We err by substituting our own goals for God's clear direction, and we miss the mark when we measure success by solely quantitative means. More than fifty years ago, some of the greatest lovers of the church were already starting to react to the church's conformity to culture. C. S. Lewis wrote: "I live in the Managerial Age, in a world of 'Admin.' The greatest evil is not now done in those sordid 'dens of crime' that Dickens loved to paint. It is not done even in concentration camps and labour camps. In those we see its final result. But it is conceived and ordered (moved, seconded, carried and minuted) in clean, carpeted, warmed, and well-lighted offices, by quiet men with white collars and cut fingernails and smooth-shaven cheeks who do not need to raise their voice."[12]

Human-Centered Optimism

Second, the Enlightenment was an era with an unrealistically optimistic view of both human nature and history. In general, people were considered self-sufficient masters of their own destiny, able to exercise their will to achieve their own goals and desires, as well as influence the destiny of others. Implicit in this optimism is the idea of progress: problems have solutions and all problems can be solved within the framework of a shared worldview. This aspect of the era became a fertile breeding ground for hatching all kinds of salvific metanarratives, or guiding stories oriented around the saving work of some person or idea. These metanarratives encompass ideas as diverse as Marxism, Fascism, and the scientific revolution. This same spirit of unquenchable optimism fueled the Modern Missions Movement.

Protestantism learned how to evangelize this kind of world. Early in the Enlightenment, the reformers observed something that, until then, had not affected people's understanding of Scripture, that by grace we are saved through faith, not as a result of our own good works but as a gift from God. This newly "discovered" ancient truth directly confronted the humanistic worldview of the day. No matter how much the human race ever accomplished, owned, paid, or invented, it would never be good enough. Salvation can only be obtained through faith in Christ and his redeeming work on the cross.

In our day, the percentage of North Americans who read and believe the Bible continues to decrease. Because other major salvific stories of the last century have failed to accomplish what they promised, they have diminished the apparent trustworthiness of ours. This means it is ever more difficult to speak into the biblical "faith versus works" dilemma that has served many generations of Christians well. We must pay attention to the reality that some other aspect of Scripture may help new generations of Christians more fully embrace their faith. This would not be the first time that the focal point from which God spoke into culture changed. The Bible tells us that the cultural heresy God called Moses to speak into was idol worship, and the cultural problem Paul most effectively addressed was legalism. The church after modernism is already birthing its own reformers who will speak new meaning into the worldview of a new age. Instead of trusting imperfect humankind, as in the Enlightenment era, the church before us will need to relearn how to recenter its hope in the person of Christ.

Considering the Paradigm Before Us: What the New Worldview Is Demanding

This section is not about postmodernism. Postmodernism as a deconstructionist movement is virtually and happily dead. It is not even about *post* Modernism as a reaction to modernity. A new era is experiencing birth pangs. Its contours reflect at least two distinct responsibilities. First, the emerging worldview demands a way to help people know how to live together on and with the earth, a necessary component of living on a planet with both the instantaneous ability for global connectivity plus a never-before-realized capacity for self-destruction. Second, the new worldview insists on a response to the real scientific, social, and ecological factors that have ushered in the dawn of this new era. Leaders who cannot, for many valid reasons, make the leap it takes to minister in the context of these new realities are probably not called to design the church of the future, as the term is used in this book. As we claimed in previous chapters, not everyone is called to figure out the future. However, if your calling is to press on toward what is ahead, this next section is meant for you.

The New Worldview Must Help People Know How to Live Better Together

Several corollaries are present in helping people know how to live better together on the earth. First, the future is both global and local, and therefore the church must see itself as both. Mission and meaning for the church of the future must be large enough, and selfless enough, to encompass a planetary reality. This is not a new concept for the church, for we know our "God so loved the world," but it is a reminder of our true nature and calling. We must theologically understand the congregations of which we are a part as local interconnected communities of practice that hold a broad global definition of what it means to love your neighbor as yourself. We must also take ever more seriously the task of improving the quality of life for the poor and marginalized.

The church must model a way of life that enables humans to once again live hopefully in light of the future. Evangelicals usually interpret this to mean that people want to know that when they die they will go to heaven, and not to hell. But for many, hope means living without being beset by fear of disease, famine, the destruction of our planet, biological or nuclear war, or environmental threats. People want to know that there is a future for themselves, for their children, and for their children's children. The hope of the gospel, then, must offer God's kingdom come on earth as it is in heaven. In the emerging world, if Christians are seen as part of the solution to the problem of learning to live better on the planet, we will be invited to the table. Our challenge is to live wisely, without compromising our core beliefs.

The New Worldview Must Take into Account New Information and Realities

Second, we claimed that the worldview of this era could not ignore factors such as new scientific discovery, social realities, and ecological issues. New ways of thinking about thinking have come out of the last century of scientific and mathematical discovery, among them chaos theory, quantum physics, complexity theory, non-linear dynamics, molecular biology, and the study of living systems. These discoveries are radically shaping, and will continue to shape, how people think and act.

In his book *The Structure of Scientific Revolutions,* Thomas Kuhn first described the concept of the paradigm shift (a discontinuous revolutionary break) within the discipline and practice of science. He understood a paradigm as the achievements, values, ideas, and techniques shared by a community. He proposed that new discoveries in the sciences had the potential to lead to world-changing cultural transformation in every realm. For example, humans made the shift from hunter-gatherer to horticultural to agrarian societies in concert with new inventions such as the wheel and irrigation systems.

Business, religious, educational, scientific, and philosophical paradigms all reflect change that has taken place in the world on a deep level. Though some of these new realities are decades old, the shifts are so vast that the planet is still living in the gap. One of the more salient dimensions of the shift is related to quantum physics. In the 1920s the quantum world challenged Newtonian physics. The new science required understanding the universe at a subatomic level. This entails a worldview shift from believing that the world is predictable, quantifiable, and static to discovering it to be full of surprise, not completely quantifiable, interconnected, and less able to be controlled by humans. The most common reaction to the shift is just to try harder to create and control environments in the attempt to overcome surprise. Kuhn knew this would be the case. He quoted Max Planck's observation: "A new scientific truth does not triumph by convincing its opponents and making them see the light, but rather because its opponents eventually die, and a new generation grows up that is familiar with it."[13]

Thousands of years ago, the rebellious people of Israel sent spies to probe the new territory God had prepared for them. When those secondhand sources came back with stories about giants, the Israelites kept wandering around where they had already been and eventually died without ever entering the Promised Land. Most people today live in a wilderness story, unaware of the new and different land and uncomfortable with where it may lead. We focus on the giants and ignore God's promises. Why do some people believe that the emerging age means the demise of Christianity and the rise of Eastern religions? We believe, by contrast, that the emerging era is more compatible with biblical Christianity than most people imagine.

An Inside-Out Place to Begin: Who Versus Why

Fifteen years ago, our friend Jonathan Campbell confronted a group of church leaders who were considering the biblical purposes of the church. "When I first meet a person, I don't start the relationship by first asking about their purpose in life. I want to know about them personally, and not just their purpose for existence," he said. Jonathan's challenge was that the nature of church was a more basic question than its purpose because purpose flows from nature and not vice versa. If the church is made of people, then what should we say about people? Furthermore, if they are identified as God's people, created in His image, then the root issue is really about God. What kinds of beliefs, practices, and activities might arise if the Person of God is the place of origin for our conversation about church?

A New Metaphor

The mathematical concept of fractals offers an exciting metaphor for our investigation. Fractals are the ordinary stuff of life, embedded in creation. They are not new; they are new only to the human imagination. You understand fractals better than you think, because they are everywhere: in trees, snowflakes, rivers, ferns, cloud formations, broccoli, blood vessels, cell reproduction, and so many of the complex, multifaceted geometric patterns found in nature.

The two main characteristics of fractals are that they are self-similar and iterative (self-repetitive). In other words, a fractal is a shape made up of other shapes that pattern themselves in ever-increasing and decreasing scales. When you examine a portion of a fractal, it looks like a smaller version of a whole, and within it are other smaller versions of a similar (but usually not identical) pattern. This self-similar patterning mechanism can be found at what seems like microscopic and macroscopic levels. Zoom in or zoom out a millionfold, and the patterns are the same. Most people think about fractals in terms of solving mathematical problems or creating computer-generated art; however, a growing number of applications involve not just how fractals look, but also how they behave. Benet Mandelbrot, often called the "father of fractals," explains stock market behavior by applying fractal theory, and the critical issue for blood vessels is how the vessels are patterned to behave in the body. It is the self-similar, iterative behavior of fractals that intrigues the two of us and point us toward a way of understanding our relationship to God.

Fractals of Being

The natural world is so amazingly ordered by these fractal patterns that people who study them sometimes call fractals "thumbprints of God." His generative, self-similar repeating patterns are visible throughout creation. The book of Genesis gives us clues. On the third day, God created seed-bearing plants and trees that bear fruit with seed, according (iterative and self-similar) to their kind. On day five, He created birds and all of the creatures of the sea, each according to its kind. He blessed them, proclaiming that they were to increase in number and fill the sea and the land. On the sixth day, He created all of the animals of the earth, again, Scripture tells us, after their kind. He then made men and women in His own image, blessed them, and told them to multiply. Later in Genesis, the image of seed comes up again. His blessing on His people takes on a fractal behavior: "The land on which you lie, I give it to you and to your seed. Your seed will be like the dust of the earth; you will burst forth, to the Sea, to the east, to the north, to the Negev. All the clans of the soil will find blessing through you and through your seed!" (Gen. 28:13–14).

Fractal Patterns of Behavior

The invitation to "put on Christ" (Gal. 3:27) and be reconciled to Him is a call into intentional Self-similarity with Christ. His patterns become ours: He is the vine and we are the branches. He called us the salt and light, even as He is both of them. We note that God reconciled Paul to himself through Christ and then gave him the ministry of reconciliation. Husbands are to love their wives as Christ loves the church. We are commanded to love our neighbor as we love ourselves. The merciful are promised that they too will obtain mercy. We are blessed to be a blessing.

Conversely, we are called to break fractal patterns that do not reflect Christ-likeness. We are not to repay evil with evil. We are told to settle adversarial matters quickly, and commanded not to judge or we too will experience judgment. We practice cheek turning, and our sins are forgiven as we forgive those who have sinned against us. The eye is the lamp of the body. If our eyes are good, the whole body will be full of light. But if our eyes are bad, the whole body will be full of darkness.

A Fractal Missiology

Jesus came to them and said, "All authority in heaven and on earth has been given to me. Therefore go and make disciples of all nations, baptizing them in the name of the Father and of the Son and of the Holy Spirit, and teaching them to everything I have commanded you. And surely I am with you always, to the very end of the age" (Matt. 28:18–20).

Again, Jesus said, "Peace be with you! As the Father has sent me, I am sending you." And with that He breathed on them and said, "Receive the Holy Spirit. If you forgive anyone his sins, they are forgiven; if you do not forgive them, they are not forgiven" (John 20:21–23). "But you will receive power when the Holy Spirit comes on you; and you will be my witnesses in Jerusalem, and in all Judea and Samaria, and to the ends of the earth" (Acts 1:8).

Each of these versions of the Great Commission contains a fractal idea. In Matthew, the disciples teach followers everything (all the ways and patterns) Jesus taught them. This disciple-making pattern is generative even to the end of the age. In the book of John, Jesus says that even as the Father sent Jesus, Jesus now commissions and sends a whole new generation of followers. In Acts, the very Spirit of God in turn empowers the followers of Christ with Spirit self-similarity to transform the depth of time and space.

When we think about church, a fractal image that comes to mind is the cauliflower. A cauliflower floret looks like the whole head from which it was broken, but it is not the whole. Another piece, broken from the first floret, still takes on the material essence and patterns of the original. It too is alike in pattern and essence to that from which it was taken. This pattern continues to repeat itself over and over; the part is not the whole, but an image of it. In our metaphor, people are individually and collectively (as the church) created by God in His image of God to be and do like Him.

Who Is God, and How Does This Affect the Meaning and Mission of the Church?

In our fractal metaphor, God is both the point of origin and the whole. Unlike humans, He is inexhaustible, eternal, and omniscient. However, people are created in the image and self-similar likeness of God. Consequently, our patterns of behavior, individually and together, are supposed to reflect this reality. Let us consider just five aspects of the Divine Being that help us better understand the meaning of Church.

God Is Love

All of God's ways are love. His love is everlasting; it absolutely never fails. The Bible teaches, "Whoever does not love does not know God, because God is love" (1 John 4:8). If God's operating principle is love, then love is also the operating principle of God's church. We are called to love one another, love God, and love others tangibly. We are called to be love bearers who practice love, forgiveness, and generosity. If we do not love, no matter how large or small our churches are, no matter how great our programs are, or how much we give to missions, "if we have not love we are nothing" (1 Cor. 13:2). We are known by our love and must also be open to being loved in return.

God Is One

God is whole, fully integrated, unbroken, complete, and holy. His patterns are to complete, restore; to reconcile all things to Himself; and to unite all things in Christ. Only a few God-ordained things are called "one" in the Bible. First, God Himself (and in light of the unified Trinity, Christ Himself) is One: "Hear, O Israel: The LORD our God, the LORD is one" (Deut. 6:4). "There is but one God, the Father, from whom all things came and for whom we live; and there is but one Lord, Jesus Christ, through whom all things came and through whom we live" (1 Cor. 8:6). Second, the relationship between Jesus and God is Oneness: "I and the Father are One" (John 10:30). The relationship between a husband and wife is also distinct in its holy "oneness": "For this reason a man will leave his father and mother and be united to his wife, and they will become one flesh" (Gen. 2:24). Finally, Jesus prayed that the followers would be one: "I pray also for those who will believe in me through their message, that all of them may be one, Father, just as you are in me and I am in you" (John 17:20–21). Jesus prayed for the unity of His disciples: "May they be brought to complete unity to let the world know that you sent me and have loved them even as you have loved me" (John 17:23).

Jesus, then, asks His followers to pattern themselves after His own Oneness. We engage in kingdom acts that redeem and restore such as forgiveness, reconciliation, justice, creation care, healing ministries, peacekeeping, race relations, and ministry to the powerless. Through His Spirit, we learn to be whole, healed, and restored, and we also help others experience this (John 17:11). Reconciliation and healing is a clear function of a Church patterned in the image and likeness of God.

God Is the Creator

God is the life-giving Creator/Designer of everything that exists. He creates in His image, sustains what He creates, and as Creator of the universe His perspective as cosmic God has placed His creative Holy Spirit in us; therefore we are creative by nature. Individually and together as the church we are generative; we create and we reproduce together not as a reflection of our own genius but as reflectors of God's goodness, generosity, and beauty. We create things that reveal God and make Him known, thus helping people to connect heaven and earth. We respect what God has created to the extent that we honor His long-range perspective of creation.

God Is Light

The Scriptures teach us that God is light. Light is the only scientifically acknowledged absolute in the physical world. God is absolute, and He is truth. He is radiant, revealed, and revealing. Light intercepts and dispels darkness. It makes known that which is unknown. Jesus is the light of the world and in turn calls us as light, to allow our light to shine before others. We acknowledge and worship the King and His kingdom, make Him known, know each other, know and allow ourselves to be known, and live openly before God and others. The church is radiant, transformational, and missional by nature, and not simply by purpose or quest.

God Is Relational Within Himself

God is the Creator-community of Father, Son, and Spirit, the three in One. He is the image of unity in diversity, and the model for true community. In recent decades, the church has widely acknowledged this concept. One great contribution of the first Lausanne Congress is that it saw the church in terms of community and the people of God. Vatican 2 referred to "the people of God on pilgrimage at the service of the world."[14] We are called to be a relationally based spiritual community created in the image of the Trinity, drawn together by spirit and the person of Christ, led by the abiding Spirit (through listening and prayer) and created in self-similarity to God. We engage in His activity, connecting with each other in ways that help us practice living openly and honestly.

If we understood just these few basic characteristics of the person of God, how would it define our lives as followers of Christ? Linda often assigns students to spend a week practicing just one aspect of His Personhood—oneness, for example. She calls her class into conscious behavior that models and reflects the Christ-filled meaning of One. All things that work toward oneness are acceptable (such as reconciliation, forgiveness, sharing with others), while those things that work against oneness are to be self-corrected (selfishness, narcissism, judging others, unforgiveness). It is a challenging experience for most; we fall so short. If we truly practiced becoming fractals of the Trinity, what would we know, and what would we be and do differently as a result? Can the church live missionally, purposefully, worshipfully, and in honoring relationships with God and people if we faithfully live into the fractal principle?

5

DESIGNING AROUND BELIEFS

What would an understanding of the church (an ecclesiology) look like if it were truly missional in design and definition?
—GUDER AND BARRETT, IN *MISSIONAL CHURCH*[1]

THEY CALLED IT THE ENLIGHTENMENT—the age of information. In that era the world is fast leaving behind, people began thinking of church as a place where they would go to be fed information to help them in their spiritual pilgrimage. When spiritual growth didn't happen as expected, better information transferal systems became common: sermon notes were meant to be digested over the week, outlines and alliterative devices triggered memory, discipleship books became surrogate mentors, and midweek Bible studies replaced family time or neighbor time. Education led congregants to right doctrine and, theoretically, to right practice.

As a result, the best leaders were not only highly educated but also highly gifted communicators who could help churchgoers absorb the necessary information. Naturally, this situation fostered an understanding of church that was oriented more toward knowledge than practice. Believing and doing became separate activities. In this chapter, we seek to reconnect these concepts by considering believing as an active verb. Christian beliefs are expressions of faithfulness that go beyond what we think and say, to how we live out our shared commitment to Christ.

Even when they do not realize it, churches live out of their core beliefs and passions. What they really believe is written all over their practices, activities, programs, and leadership choices. It is reflected in the stories they tell most often, in the songs they love to sing, and in how they invest time and money. When you think about it this way, what do you really believe about the church? How much alignment is there between what your church intellectually or philosophically believes and the practices by which it is known?

In Chapter Four, we introduced an inside-out, systemic way of thinking about church based on the nature and activities of the triune God. This approach is not an attempt to replace a systematic approach to theology; it is merely an attempt to reflect in a fresh way. In this chapter, we continue the journey and begin addressing some practical applications. We have already discussed five aspects of God's nature. We said that He is one, He is love, He is light, He is the creator, and He is relational within God's Self. We discussed these characteristics as if they were single attributes, but we know they are not. God is not one or the other of these things at a time; He is all of them all of the time. After acknowledging that humans are not God (not omniscient, omnipresent, or infinite, and far from perfect) we continued in Chapter Four to say that people, created in God's image, individually and together as God's Church, are enabled by the Holy Spirit to reflect and echo God's character.

Our questions around this topic may be different from yours. We encourage you to frame your own ideas in accordance with what the Spirit of God is doing in your life, how you read the Bible, and your unique calling. For the two of us, three design questions arise from the immediate conversation about the nature of God. First, what do these characteristics of God say about how people *experience* His Person as they participate in the Church? Second, how do these characteristics inform the Church as it *engages* God's character and intentionally moves toward Christ-likeness? Third, how do these characteristics help the Church know how and why to help others *encounter* the kingdom of God?

Experiencing God's Person

It is possible to attend a church worship service, participate in a qualitative Christian music venue, have fellowship around a meal, hear a carefully articulated sermon, or teach others what the Bible says, and yet not experience a sense of the presence of God. In these venues, it is also possible to sense God's presence but not actually experience or be able to articulate any aspect of God's person as a result. As Christian leaders, we would like to believe we have done everything we can, and if people do not experience God in our churches then either it is their fault or they are just not ready to hear from God. This may be true; we really don't know. We spend so much time choosing the best music and pondering the right message series, because we really want God to "show up." But what are some other ways in which we can help people experience the God who is always there?

For the broken among us, what is there about our church experience that points toward a God who is whole and complete, who because He is One makes every broken thing whole again, and because He is love cares? What would it mean for a church to enter into what Scripture calls "the fellowship of Christ's suffering?" (Phil. 3:10). When one part of the Body of Christ is in pain, is that pain observed by anyone at all, or is it just not possible in the context of our goals, structures, and programs?

How can communities of faith structure themselves to help one another experience God's nature as bottomless Love? Does love apply equally to people who are less lovely, dress poorly, or earn less income, or whose behaviors do not reflect our narrow norms? What does love look like? Does our cultural understanding of a qualitative worship experience mean that the contribution of children or old people is undervalued? How do the many contexts of our being with one another as church reflect positively that, without a doubt, God is pouring His love into and through His people? What would it take for love to show up?

Are We Listening?

People who are not involved in church sometimes tell us about how they experience God, but we are not asking and we are not listening. There are thousands of ways to experience the beauty of God, yet we limit ourselves to a few. For example, people often say that they experience God best through nature. Clearly, they see something that many Christians miss. Remember the cauliflower? Nature carries the mark of its Creator, in a self-similar pattern of the original. It is not the Whole, but it does reflect the Whole in some important ways.

Many years ago, Francis Schaeffer wrote about four areas of alienation that happened as a result of the fall: alienation between humans and God, alienation from self, alienation between humans, and alienation from nature.[2] Howard Snyder notes that humans are the center, but not the circumference, for the redeeming work of God.[3] We look forward to a new heaven and earth, because we believe that Christ will restore all things some day (Acts 3:21). Biblical redemption is not only about God saving humans; it is about God in Christ saving everything. This resonates with millions as good news. If so many people experience God through nature, why not help them connect with Him in the context of nature? Why not ask *them* to help *us* connect to God in the context of nature as well?

We cannot experience God through nature if we gloss over passages of Scripture such as "the time has come for destroying those who destroy the earth" (Rev. 11:18). We forget that God's covenant is not just meant for humans: "I now establish my covenant with you and with your descendants after you and with every living creature that was with you—the birds, the livestock and all the wild animals, all those that came out of the ark with you— every living creature on earth" (Gen. 9:9–10).

We fail to acknowledge that Sabbath is given to creation and not just humanity: "When you enter the land that I am going to give you, the land itself must observe a sabbath to the LORD" (Lev. 25:2), and "Six days do your work, but on the seventh day do not work, so that your ox and your donkey may rest, and the slave born in your household, and the alien as well, may be refreshed" (Exod. 23:12). We grossly misunderstand the intent of God when we confuse the meaning of dominion with the word *control* instead of the concept of *care* or *stewardship*. Our choice to dominate and subdue the rest of nature leads to our failure to take our place alongside it. We are invited to experience God as we join in with the rest of creation in worshipping Him. What will we do with that invitation?

"But ask the animals, and they will teach you, or the birds of the air, and they will tell you; or speak to the earth, and it will teach you, or let the fish of the sea inform you. Which of all these does not know that the hand of the LORD has done this? In his hand is the life of every creature and the breath of all mankind" (Job 12:7–10).

"Praise the Lord. Praise the Lord from the heavens, praise him in the heights above. Praise him, all his angels, praise him, all his heavenly hosts. Praise him, sun and moon, praise him, all you shining stars. Praise him, you highest heavens and you waters above the skies. Let them praise the name of the Lord, for he commanded and they were created" (Psalm 148:1–5).

Engaging God's Character

How can communities of faith work together to engage God's character and become more Christ-like? The most common word for this concept is discipleship, but the church definition of discipleship is almost always individualistic. Even when discipleship happens in groups, it generally only means, "How can we help groups of individuals grow in Christ?" Instead, maybe we should ask how a church can be involved together as it identifies with the person of God in an effort to become more like Him. For example, believing that God is the Creator, how does a church encourage the collective creativity of the whole? How might it reflect God's Oneness by learning as a community what it means to practice justice, love mercy, and walk together humbly on the face of the earth (Mic. 6:8)?

Church mobilizer and parent to six children and nine foster children, Don Overstreet is also the "father" to many church planters. Many of the planters are related to Set Free, a church-starting movement among people from substance abuse backgrounds. In fourteen years, the Set Free churches have seen more than eleven thousand people go through their ranches and discipleship programs, where they switch addictions toward Jesus and away from drugs and alcohol. Besides spiritual services in many locations, Set Free members give away clothing and food and engage in many other compassionate ministries. Ron Thomas, a former crack cocaine addict, pastors the Skid Row Set Free church. Don tells Ron's story:

> Ron was digging through a trashcan in downtown Los Angeles one day when a little girl ran up to him and simply declared that God loved him. A half-hour later, a Set Free volunteer encountered Ron,

gave him an invitation to a Set Free event, and told him that he could help him out of his situation. Ron's heart responded to God; he accepted the invitation. The next day at the Set Free outreach, he broke down and asked Jesus to take his life and turn it around. In the strength of God's power and with the help of Set Free, Ron's life is healed. Now, at his outdoors church, church members give away food and clothing to hungry people whose garments smell like urine. Ron tells them how much God loves them, and they see in him the character of Christ. Every week, Ron sends approximately ten people to the Set Free ranch where they can encounter the transformational power of Christ too.[4]

It is the fractal principle at work again: Christ's person and patterns represented in His people. Here is another story:

A few years ago, Linda and five of her friends[5] began a future-church-oriented think tank which they called ReImagine. It eventually morphed into a cutting-edge San Francisco-based nonprofit organization directed by author, artist, and adventurer Mark Scandrette. The formative preorganization years shaped the six friends significantly. As they searched for shared language, several memorable metaphors arose. One was the idea of green space: over the months a repetitive theme was appreciation of San Francisco's justice-oriented, earth-keeping, peace-loving culture. These things seemed to reflect aspects of God's character, even though in most cases there was no visible sign of Jesus. Most local churches lacked this activist spirit, and even seemed to miss out on some of the wonder of the nature of God as a result. Nevertheless, these churches were still places of beauty and worship. Our hearts longed for a merging of these two streams.

One day Dieter Zander, a member of our group, stood at a whiteboard emphatically waving a green marker, talking about the meaning of life in the kingdom of God in terms of "righteousness, peace, and joy in the Holy Spirit" (Rom. 14:17). When Dieter drew a green mark, it dawned on Linda that the color is composed of yellow and blue. We named the Christian's path toward life in Christ "the yellow journey" and the activist's path the "blue journey." From that day on, the friends began imagining "green space" that brought together both recognition of Jesus and concern for things usually outside the scope of our particular Christian traditions. We knew that blue journey people have a difficult time picturing themselves in yellow spaces, and that most followers of Jesus have an equally difficult time with what we called blue space. The alternative was to engage God's character by creating green space everywhere. Our vision for San Francisco was (and is) that it become vibrantly green.

Who and what are the potential carriers of green DNA? We think they include churches, businesses, nonprofits, hospitals, families, individuals—everything and everyone. Green is transferable; it is meant to be practiced, and not simply memorized. Kenny McCord, one of the original six ReImagine leaders, started an environmentally friendly wood refinishing business and wrote his green kingdom values into the business. He and his team, which includes Dave Lantow, another ReImagine founder, are ministering God's love to hundreds of San Franciscans. Rod Washington, another ReImagine alumnus, is working with social-justice-oriented for-profits and nonprofits, working to improve the educational opportunities and the general quality of life for urban youth.

In each case, "green DNA" is helping these friends engage the character of Christ in their communities. What can you reimagine your church doing or being if it were to passionately activate, energize, and engage the character of Christ? What among the church's structure, programs, and activities (or lack thereof) helps or hinders you?

Encountering God's Kingdom

In the early 1980s, Howard Snyder wrote to awaken the church to God's kingdom priorities:

> In church business, people are concerned with church activities, religious behavior and spiritual things. In the kingdom business, people are concerned with kingdom activities, all human behavior and everything God has made, visible and invisible. Kingdom people see human affairs as saturated with spiritual meaning and kingdom significance. Kingdom people see first the kingdom of God and its justice; church people often put church work above concern of justice, mercy and truth. Church people think about how to get people into the church; Kingdom people think about how to get the

church into the world. Church people worry that the world might change the Church; Kingdom people work to see the church change the world. When Christians put the church ahead of the kingdom, they settle for the status quo and their own kind of people. When they catch a vision of the kingdom of God, their sight shifts to the poor, the orphan, the widow, the refugee. . . . They see the life and work of the church from the perspective of the kingdom. If the church has one great need, it is this: To be set free for the kingdom of God, to be liberated from itself as it has become in order to be itself as God intends. The church must be freed to participate fully in the economy of God.[6]

Today, the church in the West is beginning to rediscover the centrality of the message of the kingdom of God, and it is influencing God's people in a big way. The voices have become many, they are significant, and they are urgent. The questions that distinguish this conversation, such as the ones addressed next, are paradigm-shaping.

Church-Based or Kingdom-Based Ecclesiology?

Del Cerro Baptist Church in San Diego County successfully planted at least one new church every year from 1986 to 1995, while at the same time growing from four hundred to more than one thousand in attendance at their main site with a building that seated fewer than three hundred. They started churches and outreach ministries in five languages and began churches in apartment complexes, mobile home parks, new master planned communities, a movie theatre, and more. Every time a new church started, Del Cerro gave people and money to it, in addition to employing Linda as their full time Minister of Church Extension. A few months after a new church began, Del Cerro's members wanted to know when and where the next church would start, and how they could help make it happen.

Senior Pastor Sam Williams led the church to give sacrificially to these new churches because he fundamentally believed that "corporately, as well as individually, it is more blessed to give than it is to receive." Linda had no church growth category for Sam's ideas about starting multiple churches. It would have been easy for Del Cerro to stop planting churches and build a larger sanctuary, which is what common wisdom advised.

Linda remembers the day she finally realized what made Sam Williams and Del Cerro Church different: they were simply more interested in God's kingdom than their own. It happened in 1999 when Sam (by then a seminary professor) asked Linda to coteach a church planting class with her friend Dieter. Dieter selected Dallas Willard's *Divine Conspiracy* as a text, and Linda chose Guder and Barrett's seminal work *Missional Church*. Like two bookends, *Divine Conspiracy* called for personal commitment and *Missional Church* called for a church-based renewal around Jesus' message of the kingdom of God. Remembering and re-aligning around these words changed both Linda's and Dieter's lives.

> After John was put in prison, Jesus went into Galilee, proclaiming the good news of God. "The time has come," he said. "The kingdom of God is near. Repent and believe the good news!" (Mark 1:14–15).

> I must preach the good news of the kingdom of God . . . because that is why I was sent (Luke 4:43).

> But seek first his kingdom and his righteousness, and all these things will be given to you as well (Matt. 6:33).

> Your Kingdom come, your will be done, on earth as in heaven (Matt. 6:10).

Missions Programs or a Missional Theology?

Today's church has posed itself a serious challenge: to live according to its missional nature rather than simply organize around mission activities. This challenge is something of an antidote to the church's previous practice of piecing together a theology out of the two "Great Commission" verses found in Matthew 28:18–20 and Acts 1:8 rather than from the entire biblical story. When we miss the big picture—that God is forming a people for Himself and reconciling the world to Himself—it affects our ecclesiology and reduces mission to a program or department of a church. A century ago, the German theologian Martin Kähler said that mission was "the mother of theology" in that the theologizing of the early church was necessitated by its missionary encounters with the world.[7] Over many years, other prophetic voices have tried to call us to a more authentic theology, but we have not always listened. In 1969, missiologist Heinrich Kastin wrote: "Mission was, in the early stages, more than a mere function; it was a fundamental expression of the life of the church. The beginnings of a missionary theology are therefore also the beginnings of Christian theology as such."[8]

As you design, refine, or re-align, these questions about the role of mission will be some of your most important decisions. Do you believe that missions are something that the church *does,* or that mission is something that the church intrinsically *is?* Your answer to this question either limits or releases people. It helps define whether the church seeks the lost, or whether we expect the lost to seek the church. Which will it be?

"Present Tense" or "Present/Future Tense" Mission?

"Mission" in Western civilization needs to assume a posture of responsibility toward future generations. This is a new idea for Christians, to ask ourselves how our present actions, activities, and decisions may affect future generations of Christians. The word for this is "sustainability." Consider these words attributed to Aristotle: "A barbaric culture consumes all of its resources for the present; Whereas a civilized culture preserves them for later generations."[9] What then, are the resources that the Church is consuming?

We are consuming the harvest without reseeding. Soon after Linda and her family moved to San Francisco, she remembers hearing a Southern Baptist evangelist warn, "We are a harvesting-oriented denomination in the midst of an unseeded generation." He explained that Southern Baptists (as well as other Christian groups) were evangelizing people whom they knew best how to reach, and ignoring everyone else. This was a groundbreaking revelation. Most of the churches the two of us worked with as church planters and strategists used methodologies that were gleaned from the lowest-hanging branches, growing their congregations by attracting people who were the most likely to attend a new church in their neighborhood. These churches operated unsustainably; they relied on marketing-type strategies, such as mailing out information about the church, but almost never reinvested themselves in the community by sowing seeds from which they themselves would never benefit—as with prayer for the communities' future, or actively serving in ways that would authentically and positively represent Christ to neighborhoods. Over the years, as Christians reap where they do not sow blessing, it has yielded fallow soil.

All of these kinds of decisions and more are communicated not just through words but also in our structures, methods, paradigms, and programs. There are so many questions to ask; what are yours? What does a church look like when it is modeled on the ministry of the Spirit? How would a staff team be structured if it fully believed that Jesus modeled sacrificial, servant leadership? What could a church's budget or building say about its concern for the poor? Does your church really believe that every follower of Christ is given gifts by the Spirit that are available to the body? Everyone? Really? Where does the Spirit enter into church decision-making processes or leadership selection? Who is a "quality" person your church might pursue for membership? Who receives preferential parking privileges? What issues capture your church's passion enough to spark a heated discussion? What would be different if we believed that God the Father, Jesus, and the Holy Spirit were really in our midst? What do you really want people to know about God and about His people, and how is the church learning to say that without words?

6
RELEASING COMMUNITAS

It is not from ourselves that we learn to be better than we are.
—WENDELL BERRY, "THE LOSS OF THE FUTURE"[1]

ALLAN'S FAMILY IS A PART of a church network in Colorado that has recently planted a church started among refugees from Myanmar (formerly Burma). The tribe and language of this group is called Karen. In 1812, Adoniram Judson became a missionary to the Karen people, and despite much tragedy and hardship he saw the first convert to Christ after seven years. Before Judson's death, one hundred thousand Karen converted to the Christian faith. In 1962, a military junta toppled the civilian government in the struggle to become independent of Western imperialism. The new government decided to cleanse the country of Western religion, which meant a de facto ethnic cleansing of the Karen, now perceived as a "Christian" culture. Their Christian faith is now generations old, and in several ways many in the current generation of Karen either believe they are Christian by heritage or that it is the institutional faith of their grandparents, their own version of post-Christian.

One of the young Karen women told of her village being attacked; she and her fellow villagers fled into the jungle, eluding soldiers for weeks and months before ending up in a refugee camp in Thailand, where she stayed for years before coming to Colorado. When asked her about church, she said that many people in her generation were Christian by family heritage, but that their personal faith was not alive. In fact, many had decided they weren't sure they wanted to be Christian anymore because God had allowed so much pain and tragedy in their lives. People from the Karen church have told the Karrs that occasionally the soldiers would surprise a church service "gathering" and just start shooting people. The people who were less grounded in their faith stopped wanting to "come to church." Many of the Karen say that the few who remained steady in their faith were forced to gather outside the migrating village to worship, usually in groups of only four or five, to pray, worship, study Scripture together, and encourage one another. The small groups agreed to return to their villages and encourage their friends and relatives, and to be like Jesus to them. The church Body of Christ was alive and well in that migrating community village, and later in the refugee camps in Thailand.[2] In this chapter, we want to discuss how the church is designed to be released into its macrocommunity, a concept as old as scripture and recently called *communitas*.

Becoming Communitas

Communitas is the concept that best describes the intense community spirit, the feeling of dynamic solidarity and togetherness as experienced by the Karen people throughout their refugee experience. Communitas, from a Latin noun, is encountered most frequently in the context of liminality, a threshold experience, something like a rite of passage, that qualitatively binds a group together as a vital community. Communitas generally refers to an unstructured community in which people are perceived as equals and each individual submits to the whole without losing his or her own identity. The concept has been written in anthropological circles for more than sixty years[3] and has only recently been adopted into the vocabulary of the church by several Christian social entrepreneurs. One of the primary contributors to the Christian understanding of communitas is Alan Hirsch, who conceptualizes the people of God as biblical community as they identify with one another missionally. Hirsch states, "The most vigorous forms of community are those that come together in the context of a shared ordeal or those that define themselves as a group with a mission that lies beyond themselves."[4] For Hirsch, the rallying cry of "Jesus is Lord" is the central proclamation.[5] People who are committed to one another pray together, serve one another, and in other ways live their lives out the Christ life together. As these followers of Jesus create building blocks of communitas, they naturally engage in collaborative processes that serve their microcommunities and extend organically to their macrocommunities.

God then uses their petitions to change those who are praying, resulting in a cascading momentum of transformational communitas that benefits the entire macrocommunity, including people who are not part of the local church. They just know that their neighborhood, district, town, or city has become a better place to live. Hirsch captures the spirit of communitas when he says:

> So the related ideas of liminality and *communitas* describe the dynamics of the Christian community inspired to overcome their instincts to "huddle and cuddle" and to instead form themselves around a common mission that calls them onto a dangerous journey to unknown places, a mission that calls the church to shake off its collective securities and to plunge into the world of action, where its members will experience disorientation and marginalization but also where they encounter God and one another in a new way. *Communitas* is therefore always linked with the experience of liminality. It involves adventure and movement, and it describes that unique experience of *togetherness* that only really happens among a group of people inspired by the vision of a better world who actually attempt to do something about it.[6]

Communitas, then, is a group synergy of transforming goodwill. Hirsch's interpretation is that the "togetherness" of communitas gives the group a deeper experience with God, and consequently greater courage to be the church. This is exactly what we both have discovered in the microcommunities we have experienced. It is also the principle Jesus employed when He sent His disciples out to minister in pairs, and it is what we believe is essential to the health of the present church as it seeks to fulfill God's mission.

The Leader's Role in Community and Communitas

Because of the reality of the DNA of micro- and macrocommunities, there are differences in designing church one way or another. For example, pastors see themselves as ministers to the macrocommunity or microcommunity or both. The old parish model, still practiced in rural North America today, endows pastors with the spiritual responsibility for an entire town rather than for only the "members" of the church. Today, this model is once again making sense to a new generation of both rural and urban leaders who are learning to be spiritually responsive to their larger macrocommunities. This posture also enables them to be more responsive to the myriad microcommunities, not connected by faith, that already exist in their larger communities, and to actually engage as salt and light.

It is also becoming evident that some leadership structures, notably dictatorial and institutional hierarchies, actually prevent communitas from occurring in microcommunity relationships. Communitas is sometimes tied to the traditions of an organization, but more often it is a leader not being willing to be vulnerable in this kind of transparent, intimate, and sometimes vulnerable relationship, and willing to redefine himself or herself to being accountable and vulnerable in the dynamics of microcommunity. If you are a leader, are you willing to become and release communitas?

Microcommunity Embracing Macrocommunity

When Jesus taught about loving one's neighbors, He invited His microcommunity of followers to engage in macrocommunity. In the scriptural passage where the Jewish lawyer asks Jesus for clarification about what Jesus means by *neighbor,* Jesus tells a story about a man on a journey who is attacked, robbed, and left for dead. Two church guys walk past him without checking on him, and then finally a stranger comes along who is technically the traveler's enemy. The stranger stops to help the victim. He cleans him up, bandages his wounds, and carries him on his animal to a place to be cared for; he pays for his care, including his future care. He says he will check back on him later. After telling the story, Jesus asks the lawyer the obvious question: "Which one proved to be the neighbor to the victim?" When the lawyer answers correctly that it is the man who shows mercy, Jesus says, "Go and do the same." His teaching is that neighbors, unexpectedly, extend beyond our microcommunities to those people in the macrocommunities around us. Neighbors are not necessarily those who are known, liked, or likable. These qualities are not Jesus' criteria for who He defines as a neighbor.

The biblical principle of the people of God being released into the macrocommunity is not limited to Jesus' commands, or even to the New Testament. After the fall of Jerusalem in 587–586 B.C., the Babylonians took some of the Israelites into captivity. The prophet Jeremiah wrote a letter to the people. Keep in mind that they were in exile in Babylon, living among their enemies; they were not in Judah. The prophet Jeremiah said to the people of God, "Build houses and settle down. Plant gardens and eat what they produce. Get married. Have sons and daughters. Find wives for your sons. Give your daughters to be married. Then they too can have sons and daughters. Increase your numbers there. Do not let the number of your people get smaller. Also work for the success of the city I have sent you to. Pray to the Lord for that city. If it succeeds, you too will enjoy success" (Jeremiah 29:5–7).

Throughout the Biblical story, God's heart for the nations, and the principle of releasing His people into the macrocommunity, is present.

Prayer: The Qualitative Difference in Releasing Communitas

One day, Kenny Moore, Allan's mentor and one of his closest friends, invited him to join in an experiment to pray together every day. In our society, praying every day is a logistical problem. Distance and schedules prevent physical connection. Others tried this with the Luke 10:2b prayers, with some success.[7] Allan and Kenny decided to experiment with daily prayer, even if it meant doing so on their cell phones, and even then it might mean using voicemail to record the prayer to be shared later when the message was replayed. From the beginning, the prayer was a simple request: "God, please help us understand what it means to live in our union with Christ, and teach us what it means to live in the power of the Holy Spirit." They decided to pray everyday and be open to learn what God would teach them.

For almost three years, they prayed together every day; God began to teach them, and their lives and ministries were slowly transformed. A few months into the process, they realized that part of how God was answering that prayer was that He was displaying and teaching them about His power as they connected in microcommunity. There was a synergy that began to permeate their marriages, families, close circles of friends, and even their churches. God was using Allan and Kenny's microcommunity of two with rippling effects to their macrocommunity. God also discipled them through these relationships.

Prayer as Discipleship

Allan has developed a definition of this phenomenon. We call it "Prayer Discipleship" so we can share it with others:

> "Prayer Discipleship" is a commitment of two (or more) people to pray in microcommunity every day, whether in person or by phone (or even email), understanding that the prayer opens a portal access to the transforming power of the Holy Spirit essential for our union with Christ and growth in who we are in Christ. This prayer discipleship is not dependent on outside curriculum but uses Holy Spirit's power in microcommunity in conjunction with Scripture to transform and grow followers of Jesus.

When Jesus was on earth, He lived a life empowered by the Holy Spirit through a vibrant prayer life, and He made disciples: "Again I tell you that if two of you on earth agree about anything you ask for, it will be done for you by my Father in heaven. For where two or three come together in my name, there am I with them" (Matt. 18:19–20). Another time, Jesus taught about prayer in response to a disciple's question about how to pray. He responded with a few principles and used a great analogy about having extra bread to give to those in need. Then Jesus said, "If you then, though you are evil, know how to give good gifts to your children, how much more will your heavenly Father give *the Holy Spirit* to those who ask Him?"[8] Note that the context is that Jesus was praying with His disciples (Luke 11:1) when they asked Him this question. His answer offers astounding clarity that, of course, God wants to answer His children's prayers and give them the power of the Holy Spirit they desire. Why would Jesus teach His disciples to pray a prayer that it was not in the heart of God to answer? He simply would not, so we can be confident that He wants us to pray this way.

Scriptures tell us that simply believing the right information does not equal a saving relationship with Christ. After all, Satan believed that Jesus was God's own, and the thought made even him tremble (James 2:19). Christians know and believe a lot about Jesus too. As heirs to more than a century of curriculum-based discipleship, we have a stronger base of scriptural knowledge than Christians in any other century—but this has not resulted in a stronger faith. Followers of Jesus make new disciples through developing relationships with people and telling their story about how the Holy Spirit transformed them. Believing that Scripture is authoritative, we obey God and tell others of our faith. When we talk about being a follower of Jesus, we love and help others, showing them Jesus with skin on.

Around a discipleship of prayer, churches can develop microcommunities that create communitas. Allan and Kenny Moore have practiced this together for several years. First they ask someone to join them in daily prayer, either in person or by cell phone (cell phones are even becoming available throughout the Majority World—the latest sociological term for "third world" but an attempt to rephrase it more positively because about two-thirds of the world fit into this demographic; Allan will never forget being in the Amazon and seeing many people using cell phones). These microcommunities of prayer demonstrate faith and teach theology and doctrine while opening a portal for the Holy Spirit to work. This is especially true when using scripture as the basis for teaching and correction. This approach has been effective in evangelization and disciple making, even in the most traditional understanding of these words.

In the Information Age, we developed such a dependency on written (and now video) curriculum that we can hardly fathom how to make disciples without evangelistic or discipleship materials. We rely on inductive evangelistic Bible studies, curriculum-based evangelistic Bible studies, and multimedia Bible studies such as the multilingual Jesus Video. These tools are not only costly but also still not globally accessible, and not available in heart languages (which means the first language that people think in and have spoken since their early life). Whole industries and mission agencies are now devoted to developing and reproducing effective curriculum.

In the meantime, entire people groups wait while we try to make these curricula available so that we can make disciples. Through the microcommunities of prayer mentors, Allan and Kenny are discovering that they can have a greater impact in the Kingdom of God by spending more time with fewer people, and the result is that communitas is released.

It is important to pause here to ask yourself the extent to which the concept of microcommunity encompasses what you really believe. Do you value a concept of microcommunity? Do you actually believe that prayer with a few others, gathered in the name of Jesus, has the potential to change your perspective and connect people to the transformational power of the Holy Spirit? Are you interested in the concept of prayer discipleship in the context of an intimate microcommunity? If so, this means that how you live as the church in your life will align with models that value these principles.

Missional Prayer

In 2000, while he was teaching in Vancouver, Washington, Allan shared a hotel room with a student named Jeff Simmons, who has since become a vocational missionary overseas. They doodled out a drawing that they called the harvest cycle (Figure 6.1), which was a standard explanation of missional living tied to the agricultural analogies of scripture: choosing a field, plowing, sowing, reaping, and vintaging or processing the harvest. Over the years, this image has been useful in explaining to students some key components of missional living, including extraordinary reliance on prayer and God's Sovereignty, as well as simple processes for discipling followers of Jesus. A year or so later, they added another aspect, "fertilizing," to the cycle between "plowing" and "sowing." In the analogy, the soil is the hearts of people who need their lives transformed by God's Spirit. No human can "turn the soil" of another person's heart to be open to spiritual issues; only God can do that. However, the plowing means that we depend heavily on praying for people and macrocommunities that we love, and that God answers how God wants to, but we recognize that by praying God changes us. Prayer is a catalyst for love. It initiates a cycle of loving more, caring more, and responding to others in more Christ-like ways.

FIGURE 6.1. HARVEST CYCLE.

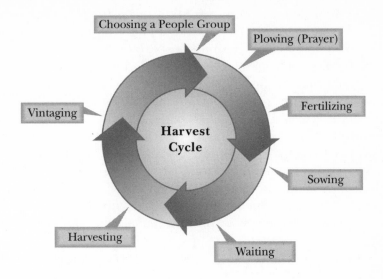

Get Dirty

There is another missiological principle at work here. One of the best things a farmer can do to prepare the field for new seed is to fertilize the soil. Allan often asks his classes, "What organic material can be spread on the soil of needy hearts to make them more fertile to receive the seed of the gospel?" Someone usually says "love" or "service," or something similar. Allan will ask who does that, and finally will have to blurt out, "Followers of Jesus are the organic material that gets mixed into the soil as fertilizer. The church is the poop!" Students laugh and start taking notes furiously but begin to realize that they are the poop that God wants to mix into the soil of the macrocommunity to make it more fertile for the Kingdom. Once when Allan was working in Ukraine, he was teaching this and the translator balked when the poop statement was made. The translator was unwilling to say to the class that the professor had just called them all "poop." In the mind of the female translator, the concept of Christians being called "poop" probably goes against the church culture's impression of ourselves as Christians in general, and it may have been too blunt for good intercultural communication.

To understand the implications of this principle, a follow-up analogy is needed. If a farmer had a large field and hauled in a tractor-trailer load of manure and dumped it on one corner of the field, would the field be fertilized? The obvious answer is no. The corner of the field with the pile of manure would be ruined. The rest of the field would have no benefit at all and in some regards would be worse off, because of the smell of the pile of poop. This is often what we do. We pile up all the organic material (the Christians) in one pile over in the corner of the community. We call it church and then we say the community is being reached. In reality, from the perspective of the "field," all that's there is a big stinking pile of poop that is ruining the field for everyone. From a church culture perspective, we think we are helping, but from a macrocommunity perspective we are at best smelly, and at worst destructive. If, however, you spread the pile of poop all over the field, over time the poop mixes with the soil, the smell goes away, and the soil is more fertile.

For Whom Does the Church Exist?

In Chapter Three we claimed that macrocommunity includes the people in our cities or communities who make up the neighborspheres of our everyday existence. We know them from our neighborhoods, work places, schools, clubs, banks, and grocery stores. They are the people whose life trajectories incidentally intersect ours: casual acquaintances who invite us to be Facebook "friends," neighbors we wave to as we drive our cars into the garage, and church members whom we seldom encounter outside of a casual handshake or attentive nod during Sunday's slotted time of greeting. We are glad for our microcommunities, but we vaguely sense that they could be better. What are we waiting for?

Because our lives are already filled with church activities, neighbor-sphere friendships continuously elude us. However, when Jesus talked about our becoming salt and light, it was not the microcommunity but the macrocommunity of which He spoke. It matters that we figure out how to engage and participate in our larger communities in a healthy way. Being good is not enough; it is a poor imitation for doing good toward others. The fact that such a small percentage of church members, including leaders, have so little time for people outside their own small groups means that something is not working. There are some key design questions every church answers either intentionally or by default:

- For whom does this church exist?
- Who is my neighbor?
- To whom does Jesus require His followers to extend love?

One way to respond to the question, "For whom does this church exist?" is to contend that every church exists to glorify God, but it must also be asked, "For whom *else* does it exist?" We say that it exists for "us" when we direct all of the resources, energy, volunteer, and staff time ministering to those already on the inside. Pastors, for example, must decide whether they are pastors only of church members, or if they also pastor a town or neighborhood where the church exists. Churches will either recognize and value members who use their spiritual gifts to serve communities, or they will notice and appreciate only those who serve members. On the other hand, some churches will respond that the church exists for "them." In this case, "them" means a macrocommunity of people who do not fit our criteria of being followers of Jesus. In such churches, resources are directed outward, moving the macrocommunity toward the inside, that they may become like us. In extreme cases, community is reduced to fellowship and fellowship is reduced to a byproduct of evangelism.

We need to ask ourselves some serious questions at this point. Do we individually and as microcommunities choose to align our lives in such a way that we intentionally engage our macrocommunities? Does our concept of the work of God allow us to focus more on the holistic transformation of our macrocommunities, or are we comfortable confining our activity to the wellbeing of our local church communities? The answers to these questions factor into design decisions.

The Story of Ethne

Ethne Church Network is one example of a network of churches that has chosen to move past the barriers of "us" and "them." They started meeting in Allan and Kathy Karr's home, and taking community really seriously. Ethne dreamed of a day when there would be a network of autonomous churches all reflecting the church value that its mission was meant for *panta ta ethne* (all the nations or people groups). Started in 2002, in six years Ethne planted more than twenty churches of different models. One-third of them meet in homes, as in the Karrs' house, and the rest represent various other models. They include the church among Karen refugees, Mongolians, Pakistanis, Zambians, bikers, cowboy ranchers, Hispanics, Romanians, Caucasians, and others. A small house church of around thirty people sponsored all of them. Thus, Ethne plants churches for "us" and churches for "them." They are discovering a way of releasing communitas into the macrocommunity, and to simultaneously help form new microcommunities.

The Nidus Way: Nurture and Release

A few years ago, Linda was meeting with two church planters, Robert and Ryan, who were also social entrepreneurs. They were trying to conceive an organization that would be friendly to the planet, nurture healthy microcommunity, and furnish a financial platform for a network of church planters in the Bay Area. Linda evolved the idea of a nest as a way of thinking about how to do this. Originally considering the concept of an umbrella network, Linda realized that an umbrella turned upside down resembles a nest. Nests are the places of birth, nurture, development, and eventually and most importantly release. The team selected a name that attempted to capture this meaning: "Nidus: The Latin word for 'nest,' nidus is used in medicine to refer to any structure that resembles a nest in appearance or function."[9] In nature, this is normative and positive. It is good, for example, that birds are nurtured until they are ready to take care of their own needs, and it is also good when they are released to be fully mature contributors in the ecosystem. In the same way, it is both positive and normative when communities function as communitas, released naturally to make an investment in the macrocommunity.

Macrocommunities and Neighbor-Spheres

Also few years ago, Linda and some colleagues surveyed their city and found among nonreligious people a common theme: traditional religious institutions that owned buildings were seen as "parasites" to the community. The accusation was based on several observations. First, they knew that churches owned prime business properties; benefited from police and fire protection, roads, and other public amenities; and yet paid no taxes. Second, sometimes people who had previously served the macrocommunity with their time and money stopped their significant civic engagement when they became church or synagogue members. Instead, they gave everything to their religious organizations. These same people gave money through their church groups to broader religious causes, like world hunger or other relief needs, but it just did not transfer into local awareness.

There are two ways churches can have an impact in their neighbor-spheres. One way is when a macrocommunity of faith acts generously to offer a product or a service and invites the public into their space to use it. We are familiar with gymnasiums, food banks, clothing pantries, parenting courses, sports leagues, community centers, recycling programs, rehab programs, book clubs, and so forth. Practically, this usually happens when a large macrocommunity of faith invites people who are not members of their group onto their church campus. There are many healthy examples of churches that offer themselves as a resource to serve their macrocommunity. There are also examples of churches that deliver service to communities not as an end in itself but as a way to promote the church. It is not always easy to find the line between serving others and serving self. With these strategies, the design needs to include a gathering place, and a way to market the church for people to gather.

The second way that churches as macrocommunities of faith can have an impact is by understanding and acting according to their intended nature. We are the sent people of God who are called to leave the gathering in order to serve. Madeleine L'Engle wrote, "My moments of being most complete, most integrated, have come either in complete solitude or when I am being part of a body made up of many people going in the same direction."[10] We imagine the church as part of a wonderful, serving community of faith.

A few years ago, a survey at BayMarin Church in San Rafael, California, showed that most members also volunteered in some capacity in their larger macrocommunities. Recently, working with other local churches, the congregation organized a Parks

Clean-Up day. Four hundred church people represented several local churches. They put in a hard day of work, giving thousands of dollars to the Parks and Recreation department to take care of needed improvements. The very next day, the *Marin Independent Journal* reported:

> Evangelical churches are waking up to the fact that we need to serve the community and not just talk about it," said David Cobia, lead pastor of Bay Marin Community Church. "We felt like we needed to bring down the walls between our churches and do something for the community that was just pure service." He and other pastors have been getting together for some time to brainstorm projects that their congregations could take on as a unified group. Saturday's parks cleanup was the first in what they intend to be a series of community-oriented activities.[11]

As the director of Page Street Center, part of Eric Bergquist's job is to help Christians overcome their tendency to huddle. When they are assembled in large or small groups, they become aware of biblical perspectives on things like injustice, poverty, and service. They leave gatherings to visit Page Street, and to practice those values, feeding the hungry, showing kindness, being generous with their time and resources, and advocating for the needs of others. Eric is reminded that during football games teams are called together, as necessary, to form huddles. In these huddles, the players communicate important information, strategize next moves, and celebrate victories. The point of the game, though, is not the huddle. The measure of being "called together" is largely seen as the players are "sent out."

What, in your opinion, is the value of assembling? How do you live well in your neighbor-spheres? If we take both microcommunity and macrocommunity seriously, what are some ways to bridge the gap? What kinds of church organizational design are conducive to healthy micro- and macrocommunities? What needs to be included in your design to ensure that communitas is released?

The Emerging Value of Collaboration

Coordinated by the U.S. Department of Energy and the National Institutes of Health, the Human Genome Project was a worldwide collaborative project that mapped all the genes and gene sequences in human DNA. A collaborative encyclopedia called Wikipedia was launched in 2001. Its Community Portal page reads: "This is the place to find out what is happening on Wikipedia. Learn what tasks need to be done, what groups there are to join, and get or post news about recent events or current activities taking place on Wikipedia."[12] Wikipedia extends the invitation for everyone who uses the site to be both gleaner and creator of what is becoming an excellent free encyclopedia.

This massive effort was possible, in part, because of Linus Torveld's "Linux Kernel," the key to a computer operating system that would propel the free software movement conceived in 1983 by Richard Stallman. The free software movement protected the rights of users to study, modify, copy, and share programs in ways that benefit the whole community. Out of it the Creative Commons movement was birthed. This includes portals, aggregation and archives such as Flickr, Internet Archive, and Wikimedia Commons; formal publications and instructional materials such as MIT OpenCourseWare, Clinical Second Life, and Open Wikieductor; collaborative content such as Wikinews, Wikitravel, and Uncyclopedia; plus free Creative Commons blog hosting services such as Wordpress.com, Blogger, and Typepad.

These are all symptoms of what Thomas Friedman wrote about in his 2005 best seller *The World Is Flat*.[13] He believed that it *was* globalization that leveled or "flattened" the playing field in business and economics. This leveling or flattening has been observed in all aspects of society and culture. There is a demand for new leadership structures and new ways of working together. A flat world demands a more level playing field, a reality that has huge implications for how organizations, including churches, structure themselves. One of the new design tasks of today's church is to learn how to create contextually relevant, biblical structures that serve this new kind of world. Maybe you and your friends will help co-create a fresh expression of church, a released communitas. Maybe, together, you will discover an even more biblically consistent paradigm in the process. Are you in?

7

DESIGNING IN CULTURE

We don't see things as they are. We see things as we are.
—Talmud (but made famous by Anais Nin)

On March 12, 2007, the *Times Online* (UK) published a news story about a professional adventurer, Col. John Blashford-Snell, titled "Church Organist Required for Jungle Meteorite Hunt."[1] This excerpt fascinated us:

> [Blashford-Snell, who] made headlines in 2000 when he took a grand piano 350 miles (560km) along the Amazon River as a present for the Wai Wai tribe in Guyana, intends to deliver a pedal organ to the isolated Ojaki community as a way of persuading its people to help his expedition.
>
> The colonel's team, which will also help to install a clean water supply and perform medical duties for the Ojaki people, are reliant on local expertise to build bridges to the [meteor] impact site, which is five miles wide. The locals are religious and have asked the visitors to install an organ in their newly built church.
>
> The organ—a pedal-powered Harmonium donated by St. James's church in Milton Abbas, Dorset—will be flown to La Paz and then transported by lorry 120 miles over the Andes to the Beni River. It will then be loaded onto a 59ft (18m) boat for a 430-mile journey over rapids and more dangerous manmade hazards.[2]

In a follow-up article on August 16 of that year, the *Times Online* reported on the delivery of the organ:

> It was loaded on to a 15-metre boat and guided past treacherous logjams until it reached the Ojaki village. "We put the organ back on its sledge and with the help of the villagers we pulled it up a steep slope," Colonel Blashford-Snell said. "We opened it to make sure it hadn't broken and immediately one of the organists we had brought with us jumped on it. In no time the sound of Bach's Toccata and Fugue [in D Minor] was playing over the village."

> Claire Roff, 33, a professional violinist, helped to teach the villagers how to play the organ. "The first few days I demonstrated it to the village, because they had never seen anything like it," she said. "The village president chose three women to learn to play it. One woman, called Nelly, did very well. At the end of the four weeks she was able to play for a service in the church."[3]

Why did the Ojaki tribe in the jungles of Bolivia think they needed an organ? Who told them this was better than their indigenous musicology?

Here is another, very different story about culture. The story of Ruth and Naomi is a captivating account about two women bound to one another despite differences in age and culture. When Ruth's husband dies, Naomi decides to return to her homeland. Ruth helps Naomi make the voyage, but when she fulfills her obligation, instead of returning to her own people and culture she displays unyielding loyalty: "Don't urge me to leave you or to turn back from you. Where you go I will go, and where you stay I will stay. Your people will be my people and your God my God" (Ruth 1:16). A mutual, reciprocal, and loving bond emerges; Naomi becomes Ruth's mother and the grandmother of her child by Boaz. Ruth embraces Judaism and allows it to become her parent culture.

In this chapter, we talk about exegeting culture in ways that factor into both design and strategy decisions. This is the role of contextualization, a process that encourages us to understand cultures and communicate into them without compromising our faith. We use many stories in this chapter, but we revisit a few contexts over and over again because they are rich in lessons that apply to exegesis and design. We are glad and relieved to live in a time when cross-cultural principles that have been applied across the oceans for decades are finally receiving attention in North America. At the same time, we acknowledge that our own best attempts are still subject to our own cultural lenses. It seems right to us that Allan (the primary contributor to this chapter) was in Istanbul and Izmir with two of his children while writing this material. Being in this cross-cultural context heightened and magnified the significance of the content.

Understanding the Concepts

Culture

Culture can imply many things, but we use it in this chapter to mean "a shared, learned, symbolic system of values, beliefs and attitudes that shapes and influences perception and behavior—an abstract 'mental blueprint' or 'mental code.'"[4]

Sociologist and social watchdog Daniel Yankelovich defines *culture* as an effort to provide a coherent set of answers to the existential situations that confront human beings in the passage of their lives. A genuine cultural shift is one that makes a decisive break with the shared meaning of the past. The break particularly affects those meanings that relate to the deepest questions of the purpose and nature of human life.[5]

Culture is a combination of the ideas and values and the behavior and lifestyles that result from them. It is the behavior of a person and the value reasons behind that behavior. For example, culture simultaneously shapes and is shaped by its language. Language learning is partially about learning the culture that is imbedded in it. When learners actually begin to think in their new languages, they are on their way to becoming indigenized. Culture is also an identity-shaping way of life. Our friend William Nathaniel was raised in India. For Christians, eating beef was permitted, but as an Indian he can never really allow himself to enjoy eating cow. Even after living in the United States for ten years and graduating from a doctoral program here, William eats Indian food, and he worships best sitting on a mat beating an Indian drum. Additionally, he hasn't adopted American adherence to schedules and operates on a more flexible time sense. But William is more than an Indian Christian; India is a big place. William is from Luchnow, a city that is famous for being extraordinarily polite. All of these factors help to shape his cultural identity.

From Aristotle to Aquinas, it has been theorized throughout history that human beings are born with a *tabula rasa* (blank slate mind, no innate mental content) and that knowledge and behavior were the result of exposure to some environment. This concept spilled over into the old missionary approach to culture that suggested there was nothing about non-Christian culture that could be built on. The approach of the day was to wipe the slate as clean as possible of all cultural ideas and practices so that a new "Christian" culture could be built from the ground up. It was not only Christendom that committed cultural genocide. The practice from which it arose was a phenomenon attributable to hundreds of years of Western exploitation and conquest. Yet there are aspects of almost any culture that reflect some aspects of the Kingdom of God. Is the culture a spiritual one? Is it open to prayer? Are its people oriented around community? Are they gift givers? Are they a just and caring people? What do those things look like in the culture about which you are thinking?

Worldview

Worldview is a term widely used in the social sciences and humanities, particularly in anthropology and in philosophy. For the purposes of this chapter, we work with a definition proposed by anthropologist James Sire: "A worldview is a commitment, a fundamental orientation of the heart, that can be expressed as a story or in a set of presuppositions (assumptions that may be true, partially true, or entirely false) which we hold (consciously or subconsciously, consistently or inconsistently) about the basic constitution of reality, and that provides the foundation on which we live and move and have our being."[6]

David Dockery advocates for followers of Jesus to be intentional to develop and live a personal worldview that is formed by biblical principles.

A Chinese proverb says, "If you want to know what water is, don't ask the fish." Water is the sum and substance of the world in which the fish is immersed. The fish may not reflect on its own environment until suddenly it is thrust onto dry land, where it struggles for life. Then it realizes that water provides its sustenance.

Immersed in our environment, we have failed to take seriously the ramifications of a secular worldview. . . . What is at stake is how we understand the world in which we live? The issues are worldview issues.

Christians everywhere recognize that there is a great spiritual battle raging for the heart [sic] and minds of men and women around the globe. We now find ourselves in a cosmic struggle between a morally indifferent culture and Christian truth. Thus we need to shape a Christian worldview and life view that will help us learn to think Christianly and live out the truth of Christian faith.

The reality is that everyone has a worldview. Some worldviews are incoherent, being merely a smorgasbord of ideas from natural, supernatural, premodern, modern, and postmodern options. An examined and thoughtful worldview, however, is more than a private personal viewpoint; it is a comprehensive life system that seeks to answer the basic questions of life. A Christian worldview is not just one's personal faith expression, nor is it simply a theory. It is an all-consuming way of life applicable to all spheres of life.[7]

Worldview and culture are not the same, but they overlap each other in everyday life. Allan can drive a few miles from Denver to Boulder and meet people whose worldviews are alien to his. He can also travel across oceans and meet people from cultures completely foreign to his but who share his basic worldview. People generally attach their worldviews in one of three primary realms, as indicated in Figure 7.1. This becomes the lens through which they view the world, and out of which their intuitive questions, responses, and behaviors arise.

Worldview issues are critical in church design. Ecologically based world views yield leadership structures, participatory expectations, and community impact awareness different from those of other more "self"-centered, humanistic worldviews. For the purposes of this chapter, we ask our readers to be aware of both worldview and culture, remember that they are intertwined, and consider their implications while making design decisions. For example, hierarchical cosmologies yield hierarchical ecclesiologies, while egalitarian, participatory worldviews demand more collaborative structures.

FIGURE 7.1. WORLDVIEW CONSTRUCTION AND KINGDOM.

Spiritual Realm

God or gods?

Creator, not, or doesn't matter?

Unified or diverse?

Imminent or transcendent?

Exists, does not, doesn't matter?

Personal or impersonal?

Exhaustible or inexhaustible?

Capricious or stable?

What nature?

Is God (or gods) separate from the Created world or part of it?
How are authority and guidance mediated and for what types of things?
In what do we trust: people, the Creator, or the environment?
In a pluralistic culture, where do we begin a conversation about ethics,
and how do we construct our worldviews?

Context
(environment or social structures)

Universe or multiverse?

Good, bad, or fallen?

Is earth dead or living?

Created or life-giving and life-sustaining?

Matter, spirit, or spirit-infused matter?

Essence or pattern?

Organized or chaotic?

Controlling, controllable, controlled?

Exhaustible in eternity,
self-replenishing now?

What nature?
Cooperative or competitive?

Mechanistic or organic?

People

Created essentially good, evil, fallen,
or neutral?

What motivates their decisions?

In what do they believe or trust?

What are mortality and immortality?

How to relate to self and others?

Are they equal or not equal?

Are some people perfect,
incapable of sin, or not?

How to relate to spirit world?

How do and can they relate to their
context?

Can people change and be transformed?

Of what nature?
Cooperative or competitive?

What makes a person good/righteous?

Does your own worldview value age-honored traditions of other cultures, or see them as challenges to overcome?

People Group

Jesus said to go and make disciples of "all the nations," or in Greek (as we saw in Chapter Six) panta ta ethne (Matt. 28:18–20).

Ethne is the Greek word from which we derive the word ethnicity. The peoples of the world are not neatly arranged geopolitically but are identified, defined, and scattered in myriad ways. Lausanne offers the following definition of people group: "For evangelization purposes, a people group is the largest group within which the Gospel can spread as a church planting movement without encountering barriers of understanding or acceptance."[8] In the twenty-first century, however, with more than 50 percent of the world's population living in complex urban settings, this definition is still inadequate.

Sociologists talk about another way in which people group themselves; they identify with one another on the basis of kinship (family, band, neotribe), affinity (language, culture, interest, vocation), or geography (my town, neighborhood, apartment complex). It actually doesn't matter so much how the concept of people groups is defined as it does to be conscious that they do. For example, what does it mean to be young, urban, and Caucasian or Latino or Asian or African American? Does it mean stockbroker, artist, felon, or geek? In Oakland, Chicago, or Detroit, any of those ethnicities could form their own group. The question could be asked another way. What does it mean to be a young stockbroker, artist, felon, or geek living in Oakland? It could also mean Caucasian, Latino, Asian, or African American. People simply identify and group themselves in multiple ways.

What Is Microculture?

In pluralistic societies like those of North America, it is normative for many cultures and subcultures (macrocultures) to exist simultaneously, often intermingling, together creating the charm of a larger indigenous (macro) culture. San Diego is influenced by Mexico, and Miami is influenced by Cuba. The names of their streets, the local cuisine, how holidays are celebrated, and the whole flavor of these cities say that it would be impossible to detach them from their Latin influence. What is microculture? Within a wider general culture, there exist small units of culture that retain identity and traits not lost to the assimilation of a specific people within a dominant culture; a small subculture.[9] A microculture (racial, religious, or social) includes customary beliefs, material traits, and social forms. Macroculture, then, is the dominant culture in a society.

It controls the power, writes the rules and laws, and owns or controls the resources. When the Bergquists moved to San Francisco, they lived in the Sunset district, a neighborhood filled with Chinese-owned businesses. Linda noticed that when she visited the crowded bakeries, she often waited seemingly unnoticed while many others came and left. What was happening? Linda could believe that the bakery employees did not want or like her; she could stay away from these businesses, or she could try to figure it out. She discovered that when she learned the names of the pastries she wanted (like *har gow* and *siu mai*), she was served as quickly as anyone else. Despite the fact that her own culture was the macroculture, Linda needed to learn words in the language of the dominant microculture to thrive in that neighborhood.

Three Kinds of Relationships to Cultures

Every ministry team has a relationship to its culture, ranging from stranger, outsider, or missionary all the way to native, insider, indigenous. Sometimes it is possible and preferable to become indigenized, but sometimes it is neither. How indigenous are you to the people to whom God has called you? Are you living as a cultural insider or not? Finally, to what culture(s) are you an insider? The culture of your city? your region? your church? your place of origin? In each situation, we need God to grant new eyes to see.

The Team Is Indigenous (Insiders) to the Culture

"Indigenous" simply means something or someone native to this place. Properly, *indigenous* is defined as "having originated in and being produced, growing, living, or occurring naturally in a particular region or environment."[10] This term can apply to plants, animals, and so on, but for this discussion we use the term in the context of how people are indigenous to a culture of a people group, lifestyle, worldview, or generation. In the transient reality of our global society, it is becoming rare to encounter a person who is living in the same place he or she was born and raised in. It is more common for people to move to new places for educational, vocational, or relational reasons, usually multiple times in their lifetime. Interestingly enough, even though people move, indigenous cultures often remain in an area. Though they do change over time, the changes occur slowly, and cities and regions keep an indigenous, even historic cultural identity.

Greenwich Village, New York; and Haight Ashbury, San Francisco, have retained their cultural reputation for years, while post-Katrina New Orleans struggles to regain its identity. An indigenous person lives out an indigenous culture. It is so imbedded into the fabric of being that it is completely natural to the person; indigenous people make indigenous decisions. They do not need to strategize to reach the culture around them because they are a product of that culture. On the other hand, in a churched culture they may be less aware of the theological problems connected to church having adapted to the culture over many years.

The best way we know to plan for indigenous churches is to raise leaders from the harvest. Indigenous leaders know how to speak redemptively into a culture because they are part of it. They don't bump into cultural barriers because their framework for making decisions is shared with the rest of their culture or subculture. Even when they cannot recognize why they like or dislike a thing, respond to it or not, their emotions speak out. Adoniram Judson first engaged Karen tribes in Burma in 1827. The first Karen convert was Ko Tha Byu, a former criminal. This passage explains the power of indigenous leadership:

> In 1828 the former Karen bandit, "whose rough, undisciplined genius, energy and zeal for Christ" had caught the notice of the missionaries, was sent south with a new missionary couple, the Boardmans, into the territory of the strongly animistic, non-Buddhist Karen. There, he was no sooner baptized then [sic] he set off into the jungle alone to preach to his fellow tribes-people. Astonishingly, he found them strangely prepared for his preaching. Their ancient oracle traditions, handed down for centuries, contained some startling echoes of the Old Testament [such that] some scholars conjecture a linkage with Jewish communities (or possibly even Nestorians) before their migrations from western China into Burma perhaps as early as the twelfth century.[11]

Judson is credited with introducing the teachings of the gospel to the Karen. He did, but it was an indigenous leader who saw the incredible spread of the Kingdom throughout this tribe.

Before Judson died, it is estimated one hundred thousand Karen had become followers of Jesus, and Judson spoke only to a few of them. As you design, do you have a plan to identify and invest in the development of new leaders who are indigenous, or at least indigenized?

The Team Is Missionary (Outsiders) to the Culture

We began this chapter with the story of the Ojaki villagers adopting the organ. That story makes us laugh, but there are hundreds like it. Starting in the early 1980s, thousands of Southeast Asian refugees were resettled in the United States. Many Lao moved to San Diego. Linda remembers visiting a Reformed church that sponsored a Laotian congregation. A bus had been sent to pick up families, but it was late returning. Instead of following a sequential geographical route, the driver had opted for what seemed logical to him: a pattern that allowed him to pick up small families first, and larger families with more children last, since they needed more time to get ready. By the time the bus arrived, the elderly Scottish leader at the church was really frustrated. "Everyone knows that God is prompt," he said. Culture.

In 1987, there were more than one hundred applicants for a church plant in the master planned community of Eastlake, in Chula Vista, California. The person who seemed right for the task was Russ Cox, who was at the time pastoring an American-born Chinese church in Northern California. Russ seemed almost right for the job in every way except one. Although he was a Caucasian, he was slight of build, and his gestures and movements seemed as if he had adapted well to his Chinese cultural environment. The church planting community was outdoors and sports-oriented, influenced largely by Latino culture. The church missions committee wondered how Russ would fit, but they believed that his capacity to adapt to one community would be transferable to another. As the interview process became more serious, however, it turned out that he was an avid sports fan and a great baseball player. One of Russ's first outreaches was to start a community baseball team. Over the years, the neighborhood drew a large Filipino constituency, which Russ could relate to because of his experience in an Asian American church. Twenty years later, the church is thriving, and Russ is still its senior pastor.

On a design level, both insiders and outsiders can minister effectively, but outsiders are more likely to make design errors unless they:

1. *Love the people and place to whom they are called.* Aaron and Tracy Monts recently moved to San Francisco to start a church. Their Facebook or Twitter status reports make us smile as they comment on coffee shops, gourmet food courts, festivals, and other activities they love about their new city. Even if they commit huge cultural faux pas, San Franciscans will still love the Monts because Aaron and Tracy love San Francisco. Is there a place or a people that God has caused you to weep over? Perhaps there are a people among whom you want to live, raise children, and connect because you love them.

2. *Have a God-given missionary gift.* Our friend "Jason" now works with Afghani Muslims in a North American context. Before being deployed as a missionary, he was evaluated formally to see if he would be a "good church starter." When asked how well he related to people different from himself, he said that he had never met anyone like that. This lowered his assessment score considerably, but we knew that his life and ministry were full of people and experiences showing he was missional to the core. He just did not see the people groups to whom he related as different from him. A favorite recent picture of Jason was taken in a barbershop in Afghanistan, where he was being shaved with a straight-edge razor. Jason loves and trusts his people group.

3. *Listen to culture.* One of Jason's greatest assets is that he listens to culture. Because he does, cultural insiders want to help him learn both the language and the culture. He has learned cultural cues that would otherwise have taken many years to glean. The same formal evaluation process that found Jason to be weak in cross-cultural skills also assessed him poorly for his entrepreneurial capacity because of his humility, which in turn has earned him the right to speak Jesus into many lives. When Cambodian refugees moved to the United States in the

early 1980s, the culture experienced a horrendous leadership vacuum. The Khmer Rouge had systematically killed all of the leaders they could find in Cambodia. Many were converted to Christianity in refugee camps, but it was really difficult to find indigenous leaders for their new churches. Even those with prior knowledge of the culture needed to listen to its changed situation. They needed to completely revisit the requirements for pastoral leadership, adopting relational and spiritual models rather than administrative and cognitive models.

4. *Possess a teachable spirit.* Alvin Toffler says, "The illiterate of the 21st century will not be those who cannot read and write, but those who cannot learn, unlearn, and relearn."[12] Despite Jesus' teaching about love, humility, and service, this is a really difficult posture for many because we assume ourselves to be teachers rather than learners.

In the summer of 2006, Allan and his family spent a month in Spain. One week, Allan's children helped an American group with a basketball camp in an upscale Alcobendes neighborhood, just north of Madrid. That same week, the World Cup championships were being played in Germany, and Spain was in the championship hunt. The camp was being held in a futbol pitch converted into a basketball court, by adding portable hoops (goals). The Americans rolled out rubber basketballs and all the children started kicking them, taking shots at the soccer goals on the pitch. The Americans running the camp screamed, "Stop kicking the balls!" After a few minutes, the director of he camp called the children into a meeting and told them that it was against the rules of basketball. Allan asked another leader, "Why don't you just play soccer on the pitch; the goals are already there?" The American leader said they couldn't play soccer because no one from their group knew how to teach soccer. Allan asked, "Why don't you let them teach you? You will still have the missionary contact you hope to have with them." The leader said, "We are the ones here to teach; we're supposed to be the experts!"

They never considered assuming the position of learner. Every time Allan goes to a culture, one of his goals is to ask an insider to teach him something new about the culture. Sometimes he asks the individual to teach him phrases in his or her language, sometimes he asks how to cook a local cuisine, and sometimes he asks how to play a new game. By becoming a learner, he can better be a teacher. Proverbs 1:5 says, "Let the wise listen and add to their learning." Being a learner is the convergence of two qualities: humility and the understanding that in order to evolve into an indigenized servant of the people group, the people have much to teach the missionary about sharing the truth with contextual relevance.

If you are a woman visiting a church gathering where it is culturally appropriate for men to sit on chairs and women to sit on the floor, will you comply? If you despise country music but are visiting a country church service, will you join in the worship? If you live in a culture that values holism and local sustainability, how might you adapt your megachurch model? What are you willing to learn, and where will you draw your line in the sand?

The Team Is Moving from a Missionary to an Indigenized Relationship with Culture

In 1996, the Bergquist family moved to San Francisco from southern California. Ever since high school, Linda had wanted to live in San Francisco, and it seemed everyone she knew thought she belonged there. In many ways, it was a great match, but as a student of culture she quickly learned that even though she dressed and spoke the part, she was clearly a nonnative. It took years for Linda and her husband, Eric, to become cultural insiders—to learn the rhythm and soul of their new city. Eventually, they began to think and communicate their faith in "San Franciscan." Their move from cultural outsiders to cultural insiders continues to evolve, and with it the potential they have to speak into the core of the city. They have finally found ways to be fully themselves, fully San Franciscans, and wholly followers of Jesus.

In the mid-1980s, many refugees from Cambodia made a series of decisions that drastically affected their futures. Wide-scale secondary migration occurred as thousands resettled from places such as Dallas-Fort Worth to Long Beach, California, and in their own words enrolled in "welfare school." Large families had more money to live on if they accepted welfare from the state of California, and possibly even worked under the table for criminally low wages. Many made this decision because they felt that if they accepted minimum wage jobs, the only ones for which they qualified, they would not have enough money to feed their families. The California-bound groups lived together in Asian communities where they never needed to assimilate. By contrast, those who stayed in Texas found jobs where they learned to communicate in English, wear Western clothing, and so on; within a few years, they bought homes in various communities. There was an exchange: loss of a Cambodian way of life for a gain in the capacity to thrive economically.

Allan moved to Colorado with his family in 1995. He still remembers immediately feeling he was born to live there—as if his whole being fit better in his new Colorado culture than he ever felt in his birth culture. He did not experience the same kind of culture shock as Linda, but he was not an insider yet, either. The word we use for both of these examples is *indigenized,* which means "to adapt beliefs, customs, etc. to local ways."[13] In this context, an indigenized leader is one who was at one time an outsider and evolved into an insider as she or he adapted, so that eventually the new culture became his or her primary culture. The result is that the leader is able to act out of an insider relationship to the culture and is capable of designing indigenous structures and forms. So how can a cultural outsider become an insider?

Getting to Know a Culture: Exegesis

Exegesis means "an explanation or critical interpretation of a text."[14] Usually, the term is used in reference to breaking down the words, phrases, sentences, and passages of Scripture word by word, or phrase by phrase, and putting them in historical and even cultural context. This same idea can be applied to aspects of culture. Figure 7.1 shows how the design process of this book integrates into the Harvest Cycle (Figure 6.1) presented in the previous chapter. In the cyclical process, exegeting the culture is important in the first cycle of design, and in subsequent cycles of reproduction (Figure 7.2).

Cultural Guides for the Journey
Informants

When cultural outsiders need help understanding their new cultures, God usually supplies informants, advisors, and people of peace. An informant is "a person who gives information; one who

FIGURE 7.2. DESIGN PROCESS.

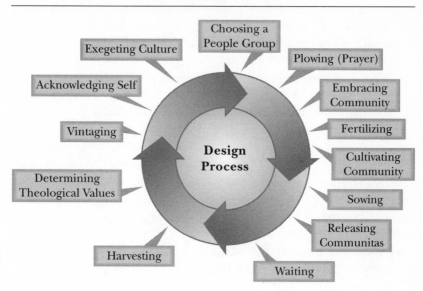

supplies cultural or linguistic data in response to interrogation by an investigator."[15] Learners need to receive informants as gifts from God and learn to recognize their gifts. Linda remembers a homeless man she met at a bus stop her first week in San Francisco. After they talked for a few minutes, the man asked, "You're a 71, aren't you?" He was correct. Many buses stopped there, but Linda was waiting for the 71 line, heading for the Sunset district. He had noticed Linda was still relatively conservative in her fashion (not her image now) because she was still new to the city and because she had her young daughter with her. The Sunset was known to be a conservative, family-oriented district. Linda skipped the next bus ride and talked with him for a long while, gleaning his grassroots knowledge of the city and its microcultures. This homeless "street sociologist" supplied valuable information about how San Francisco was organized by neighborhood, saving Linda months of research.

Third-Culture Advisors

Sometimes called a "global nomad," a third culture person is: "an individual who, having spent a significant part of the developmental years in a culture other than the parents' culture, develops a sense of relationship to all of the cultures while not having full ownership in any. Elements from each culture are incorporated into the life experience, but the sense of belonging is in relationship to others of similar experience."[16]

They integrate elements of other cultures and their own birth culture into a third culture. Because they understand aspects of both cultures, they can act as bridges between them.

Cultural Persons of Peace

Jesus gave these instructions to the seventy-two missionaries He sent out in pairs: "When you enter a house, first say, 'Peace to this house.' If a man of peace is there, your peace will rest on him; if not, it will return to you" (Luke 10:5–6). Persons of peace are culture guides and teachers who help cultural outsiders of all kinds by introducing them to the culture and its people.

Emerging Issues

Changing Worldviews

People generally anchor their worldviews in one of three places: God or gods, people (myself, tribe, humanity), or context (nature, natural world, some social construct). Although worldview shift can happen between or within any of these three, the classic biblical struggle is between God and humanity. This is evident throughout Scripture, from the garden to Babel to legalism and the faith versus works dilemma of the book of Romans.

During the last several decades, however, nature has been the default in the places in the world where modernism is rejected most strongly. With the new interest in nature came both the mythic and the mystic, an ecological worldview, and an eagerness to embrace earth-based spirituality that connected to the ideology of a benevolent, good "Mother Nature." Many Christians welcomed this shift, even New Age religions, because with it came willingness to engage in spiritual conversation. However, through a decade of devastation (earthquakes, tsunamis, hurricanes) nature proved itself to be neither compassionate nor gentle, and faith in nature is proving to be short-lived.

Meanwhile, seeking another place to land, another new worldview began to form. Not surprisingly, it is once again human-centered. This time, the conversation is about a new sort of evolved human, different from the human of the machine age, capable once again of saving the species and planet, and connected in new ways to all nonhuman life. We have noticed two opposite versions of spirituality. One assumes that humans are hyperspiritual creatures, and the other assumes the opposite. Our studies of edge cultures actually suggest that the window of opportunity for spiritual conversation is already closing. There is a new atheism rising from the ashes that may be even more challenging than what we have confronted in our lifetime.

Cultural Shifts

Globalization has huge cultural ramifications. Most people in North America are aware and appreciative of the pluralistic cultural realities in both the international community and their local neighbor-spheres. Many are curious about this new world and are eager learners. They want to learn not only *about* the other cultures but to *from* other cultures. Finally, the West is beginning to realize it has something to learn from the East and from the southern hemisphere[17] and multiculturalism is even becoming part of the Christian church landscape. In many places, single ethnicity churches are the exception rather than the norm. Our children are learning from one another, and more able to appreciate the richness of the new diversity.

Some people still believe that rapidly growing homogeneous communities are the best place for churches to thrive. Clearly, places of this kind are easier to reach and churches may grow faster in such communities. Does faster growth make for a better church, though?

In the past, this question was answered with certitude. Now, a cultural preference for diversity is shaping the edges.

8

EMBRACING CULTURE

The distance from my own culture that results
from being born by the Spirit creates a fissure in
me through which others can come in. The Spirit
unlatches the doors of my heart saying: "You are not
only you; others belong to you too."
—Miraslav Volf[1]

This chapter is about understanding and embracing culture. It is a matter of posture, rooted in a manifesto: For God so loved the world . . . and as the Father sent Jesus not to condemn but to serve and love, we are called to the same. Love is who and what we are about. It is a calling to humility, and for its sake we eagerly humble ourselves as cultural learners.

Cultural Connections

Sociologists have identified three basic ways in which people connect in culture: kinship and family, affinity, and geography. When approaching a people group as either an insider or an outsider, these three cultural connections have implications for the designer in considering how they want to structure a faith community or a church.

Kinship and Family

In Western civilization, it has been typical for family to be defined by bloodline, DNA, and marriage relationships.

Last names and inheritances have been important to us. However, we are now living in an era of history where concepts of family are being completely redefined. In Chapter Three we also discussed this issue in the context of microcommunity, but many people are now including people in their "family" who traditionally have not been defined that way. Allan has learned from tribes all over the world that *family* is defined more in the context of the village, almost what we have defined previously as microcommunity. Today, in the midst of cultural fragmentation and broken families, there is a renewed interest in church as a relational way of life. Success is being redefined in terms of health, wholeness, wellness, and relationships. Theology is being revisited in a relational framework, and it seems that, after all, it is not a bad or selfish idea to make church planting decisions in a relational way.

Over the last few years, Allan and Kathy's idea of family has changed. They used to have four children, but today that number seems to keep growing as their family opens up and others want to be part of it. Allan used to have three siblings, but more and more people define their relationship to him as "brother" or "sister"—and not in the traditional churchy terminology meaning, but like a real brother and sister. Allan and Kathy have become godparents, "uncles and aunts," and family to a lot more people than they had a few years prior. This is a way in which people connect in kinship, and for the purposes of this chapter if a designer values this kind of connection, he or she can align with the design principles given in the sections of geography discussed later.

One strategy William Nathaniel uses frequently among South Asians is a kinship-based model. Extended families, in South Asian style, gather from home to home to worship and share a meal. Whenever a home opens for *satsang* (truth-seeking community), families gather and a church is started. A Pakistani family in the Bay Area is reported to be five hundred strong. The book of Acts inspired one of Linda's friends, who is starting house churches among Chinese in Vancouver, Canada, by evangelizing whole households at a time, and helping them to immediately form churches.

Affinity

Denver has a large first-generation Romanian population that lives all over the city. Those who are church members usually commute. They leave their neighborhoods for a central location to be with their affinity group—people who speak their language and practice their customs. Affinity is a "sympathy marked by community of interest, an attraction to or liking for something."[2] This kind of connection can be based on language, subculture, first- or second-generation ethnicity, socioeconomics, lifestyle, interest, workplace, preferred worship style, a common antagonist, or any other number of things around which people naturally relate.

In the case of the Romanians, design implications include a regional strategy. Cambodian churches in California are likely to be neighborhood-based, but in Texas they are more regional. In the West, it is common to find regional nonnative megachurches made up of people who migrate from traditionally churched regions of the United States, who are looking for a church like the one they were part of back home. Though these churches do not identify themselves as affinity churches, in essence they are exactly that. Churches that address language and culture affinity are valuable on a number of levels.

Presenting the Gospel, worshipping, and praying in a heart language is an important missiological principle for engaging unreached groups. In the case of immigrants and refugees, this affinity strategy is critical, lending emotional encouragement to people who are in a new place, sometimes against their desires, and who need to connect when they gather with others like themselves for emotional health and edification. In urban settings, with the demands of work, school, and life, church may have a spiritual purpose and also serve an important function as a social gathering.

Evan is a passionate, Jesus-loving risk taker. It is only a little funny that he has a framed collection of scabs he saved from all of his early injuries. In seminary he started a surf club, and on the back of his old van he placed a specially made bumper sticker written in Greek: "Pray for Waves." After graduating, he moved to Pacific Beach, California, and planted an affinity-based church among fellow surfers. At first, his offering baskets were sand pails; sometimes services were held on the beach, and his first Sunday special guest was Skip Frye, a well-known surfboard shaper, Pacific Beach oldtimer, and serious follower of Jesus. After twelve years, the church closed its doors. We suspect that part of the problem was the volatile nature of the culture, especially one around which people relate for only a portion of their lives; affinity is not a sustainable way of relating to people over time.

Geography

In the history of the church all the way back to the New Testament, churches were identified by their geography, typically by the name of a city or a region. Biblical examples of city churches are Antioch (Acts 11:26), Philippi (Phil. 1:1), Corinth (1 Cor. 1:2), Jerusalem (Acts 8:1), and the seven city churches mentioned in Revelation (Rev. 1–3). Geographical regional church examples are Galatia (Gal. 1:1) and Macedonia (2 Cor. 8:1), among others.

Today the world is so densely populated that geographic connections include towns, subdivisions, specific apartment complexes, multifamily housing units, my neighborhood, my block. Years ago, Allan's mentor Kenny introduced him to an idea (that wasn't original to him) regarding a geographic design strategy. This strategy, thinking from a sustainable marketing perspective, stated that we needed a local church everywhere that McDonald's has decided to put in a fast-food restaurant. The idea was to balance convenience and critical mass sustainability. For people thinking to connect geographically, convenience might be a bonus, but the idea in this paradigm is to think about how to holistically be the church.

Berkeley architect Christopher Alexander, noted for his theories of design, is a paradigm pioneer. In discussing building designs, he also thinks about culture holistically:

> There is one timeless way of building. It is thousands of years old, and the same today as it has ever been. The great traditional buildings of the past, the villages and tents and temples in which man feels at home, have always been made by people who were very close to the center of this way. It is not possible to make great

buildings, or great towns, beautiful places, places where you feel
yourself, places where you feel alive, except by following this way.[3]

Alexander goes on to say that everyone needs an identifiable
spatial unit in which to belong, feel at home, and feel alive. We
agree that designing faith communities by these principles is
not only tapping into the historical pattern but also resonating
with something innate that many people groups are thirsty for
and need.

We like the idea of designing around geography because it has
such great potential to offer a kind of holistic sustainability. When
people share geographical proximity, it makes it more possible to
live in community twenty-four/seven. For the same reasons that
some people choose to eat and shop locally, those who value this as
a way of life are designing geographically local models of church.
Sometimes they live together in one house, sometimes in the same
apartment complex, and sometimes simply in the same neighborhood. They are more readily able to form missional teams that
invest in their communities. They also like the opportunity this
kind of connection affords to simplify their lives and lower their
carbon footprint by not driving to church.

Another value of geographically based ways of organizing in
some places is that it helps people to learn how to connect with
others not like themselves, in a day when the world is demanding
that we figure out how to live together with each other and the
planet. This is especially true in dense, complex areas like San
Francisco. The story about the man who guessed that Linda was
waiting for the 71 bus had nothing to do with language or ethnicity.
The Bergquists' near neighbors were Chinese, Russian, French,
Thai, Peruvian, Singaporeans, and more. This all-aged neighborhood, however, came together for many years to worship, enjoy
friendship, and celebrate holidays and life passages together. An
emerging cultural pattern of cities is that people are choosing
heterogeneity over homogeneity and messy over sterile—crossing
cultures, race, ethnicity, and socioeconomics to do so. The homogeneous strategy is viable where it exists naturally, which is true
about fewer places in North American than ever before. We are
also realizing that connecting geographically affords new opportunities for practicing Kingdom living.

Catholics have lived and congregated geographically for centuries. New language congregations (especially among people groups from a Catholic heritage such as French, Latinos, Filipinos, and Vietnamese) start within the communities of larger Catholic churches, but essentially they still practice a parish mentality. Out of this commitment, they have done a better job of holding together numerous cultures and socioeconomic groups at one time.

From the outside looking in, large cities just seem large. In reality, they are a composite of many smaller communities, neighborhoods, and barrios, each with its own identity. People within those neighborhoods have learned to manage their lives together (or want to but don't know how). Churches, synagogues, and mosques hold people together, offering a way of life that is relational and whole, more meaningful. As these cities, all kinds of towns, and their people groups continue to retribe themselves over the next decades, all of these ways of connecting will continue to play a role. Kinship-based churches are more prevalent than most people think, and even though traditional family units are challenged by numerous social forces, across many cultures people prefer family as their primary social unit.

Affinity-based groups are easier to find and join than ever. Language newspapers, television programming, online meet-up groups, and other tools make it easy to make those connections. However, consumers segment themselves in increasingly narrow ways. It takes just seconds for newcomers with no relationship to a church community to walk into a worship service and decide whether or not they belong with "these people."

If you are called to an affinity group, does it correspond with some geography too? If you are considering a geographic region: do people who live there relate to their neighbors, or do they connect with others in different ways? Do people living in this place related widely or narrowly? Is it Hope Community Church or Sunnyhill apartment complex where they most closely connect? Each way of connecting is valuable in some situations, and all three are entry ways to some kind of culture.

The Jesus Microculture

Understanding religion is a part of understanding culture. One cannot adequately understand the culture of Mexico City without understanding Latin-American Catholicism; it is impossible to understand Salt Lake without some background of the Latter Day Saints. Almost every city or region in the world can be better understood by understanding its religions. Jesus challenged His disciples to be fully immersed in their culture, and simultaneously countercultural. In one long discourse of countercultural teaching, Jesus told His disciples to carry a soldier's bag for the obligatory mile, and then carry it another mile (Matt. 5:41) At this same time, He said, "Let me tell you why you are here. You're here to be salt-seasoning that brings out the God-flavors of this earth. If you lose your saltiness, how will people taste godliness? You've lost your saltiness and will end up in the garbage. Here's another way to put it: You're here to be light, bringing out the God-colors in the world. God is not a secret to be kept. We're going public with this, as public as a city set on a hill."[4]

For many years, Christendom was the macroculture of the United States, but to follow Jesus now is to be part of a microculture. The countercultural Jesus microculture is something that brings out the God flavors and God colors in our world. It is this microculture mixed into the macroculture that creates this beauty.

Christian microcultures can either be part of what makes a macroculture truly beautiful or so countercultural that they live in tension with their macrocultures. They have the capacity to exist as salt and light, or to isolate and insulate themselves. This is an ancient practice that began when monks first began to cloister in monasteries. It later became a primary reason for religious migration. The Amish community, for example, practices isolation from the larger culture for religious purposes. Because of their quest for simplicity, they are readily identifiable. However, it is fairly common for many religious groups (not only Christians) to create their own microcultures designed for separation rather than participation. It takes only a short time for a new Christian to learn the "Christianese" language and culture. In a world that is learning to celebrate diversity as a gift from God, this practice of pulling away is doing the opposite of what we intend. Separation serves to make us less pungent and less fragrant. Why? Because most of the commands of Jesus cannot be followed unless we leave our gatherings and go embrace the people who are not part the microculture of the church.

Bounded Sets and Centered Sets

Years ago, Paul Hiebert introduced a typology about how people group themselves in churches. It has become commonly acknowledged only since his death. Here we reference just two of his set types (bounded and centered) in relationship to the capacity each has to help transcend cultural barriers (see Figure 8.1). A bounded set, as we understand it, has a well-defined boundary based on specific beliefs and practices. One biblical example of this is the apostle Paul's insistence that circumcision not be a requirement for Gentile Christians. A contemporary example might be a Christian group that frowns on dancing. To be an insider in a bounded fellowship, one would need to believe exactly the same as the group, dress like the group, and use the same buzzwords.

An alternative way for people to choose to connect is in "centered set" fellowships. These are defined by the fact that they are

FIGURE 8.1. GROUPS RELATED TO CHRISTIAN FELLOWSHIPS.

Types of Groups Related to Christian Fellowships

Bounded Groups

The fellowship is bound by membership, covenants, cultural behaviors, information, all of which decide whether the individual is "inside" or "outside" the group.
The answer to certain questions must be "correct for a person to be included."
Positional: I am a Christian, you are not.

Centered Groups

These groups form around a central organizing theme (in this case "Jesus") but unlike bounded groups they are directional (in this case "Kingdom") rather than positional. The integrated theme, transformative idea, or organizational principle holds the group together, for instance, organization around the kingdom without bounding the direction with creed or other aspects of bounded community.

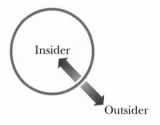

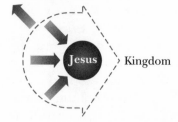

directionally focused around a significant center. Hiebert says, "A centered set is created by defining a center or reference point and the relationship of things to that center. Things related to the center belong to the set, and those not related to the center do not."[5] In the context of church, the center is a biblical acceptance of Jesus Christ and His message of the Kingdom of God. When the Jerusalem Council met around Paul's question about circumcision, it opted for a centered set of life in Christ. A decision was made to extend decision-making freedom to the new Gentile Christians, insisting on only four specific practices (Acts 15). The centered set church is not defined by right belief or practice, but by the focus on the center, Jesus and the Kingdom of God.

Here is why it matters in this conversation. When the lifestyle and values of a macroculture have a lot in common with those of a Christian microculture, it is far easier for a person outside the church to find the way in. The more bounded the church culture, the truer this becomes. Conversely, the more dissimilar the cultures, the more difficult it is for people to enter. For decades, the values and lifestyle of the church and the values and lifestyle of the macroculture in North America have drifted farther and farther apart. Not only has culture changed, but the church is also changing. This transition has been in two seemingly irreconcilable directions. First, part of the church has adopted the cultural value of tolerance and laid aside some of its former boundaries in order to adapt to culture. Second, another segment of the church has watched it happen and reacted by drawing the boundaries more closely than ever. To date, few have experimented with the possibility of centered set fellowships.

Creating Internal Cultures

Every community of faith has the opportunity to make decisions about its own culture. Many of these decisions are shaped by values, but others are made without any conscious decision-making process. One of them is a church's relationship to the outside culture. Whether a church believes itself to be indigenous to the culture or not, that church allows itself to be shaped by external cultural context or rejects it. Individual church members can be indigenous to their geography yet be so immersed in a church subculture that they do not really reflect the larger culture. Although this is certainly true about ethnolinguistic groups (such as the Chinese-born and -raised in Chinatown, New York City, who can create their own cities within a city), the same is true about Christian subcultures within larger cultures. For example, we know people born in the Pacific Northwest whose worlds are so cocooned in Bible-belt background churches that they never learn to be northwesterners. Such people are not reliable cultural informants!

Another relationship to culture is possible. William Nathaniel was raised in a poor Indian family. Missionaries gave him his first shoes. His wife, Jayashree, was born into a Brahmin family that practices voluntary simplicity. Though her father was a professor at the University of Delhi and could have lived a more affluent lifestyle, to this day he owns only two shirts and few other earthly possessions. Jayashree's mother uncharacteristically cleans not only her own home but also one where young impoverished female students stay. Though most South Asians among whom they minister in America are upper-middle-class, the Nathaniels live less easily with material wealth. In light of this, they began an Indian-style Christ satsang for mostly homeless subculture youth. Though they could never imagine themselves in a formal church, these young people sing and chant the name of Jesus in the Hindi language. (Imagine all of the layers of culture in this scenario.) But the Nathaniels are also intentionally creating an internal microculture as they gather for satsang and share their gifts of hospitality with strangers. At the same time, for the Nathaniels satsang is an act of thankfulness and remembering the goodness of God.

Earlier in this chapter, we told a story about Linda's discovery that she was less indigenous to San Francisco than she imagined. She began learning the language of her city, and still remembers the day when she realized she had learned to speak it. She was at a cafe with a friend discussing the Kingdom of God. A young woman nearby kept inching closer to listen in on the conversation. Eventually she interrupted, "What are you taking about? It's beautiful—like Eminem." To her, the language Linda used was so lovely that it reminded her of the other most beautiful thing she knew, Eminem, the Academy Award and Grammy Award–winning American rapper, record producer, and actor. Linda believes that this was the moment she knew she had learned the language well enough to consider herself an indigenized San Franciscan.

Cultural Investments in the Eternal

In the fall of 2008, Allan and two of his children visited Istanbul, where they went to the Hagia Sophia. For one thousand years, it was the largest Christian church building in the world. As the Ottoman Empire took over the city, the church was converted to a mosque, the Ayasofya, and minarets were added to call Muslims to prayer as it is scheduled each day. After Attaturk founded Turkey, the mosque was converted to a secular museum. What once was the crown jewel of Christian church buildings is now a Muslim museum. The Karrs also visited the ruins of the city of Ephesus. They stood in the theater of Acts 19, where a mob had gathered to oppose the Apostle Paul. Frightened because of Paul's demonstrated power in the name of Jesus, the people of Ephesus shouted him down, crying, "Great is Artemis of the Ephesians" for more than two hours (Acts 19:34). Paul had been so successful in Asia Minor in demonstrating the love and power of Jesus that many were threatened by the repercussions of his ministry. Ephesus, however, did turn to Jesus; later it was one of the seven churches that John wrote about in the book of Revelation. By then, it had already left its first love (Rev. 2:4).

None of those seven churches or any others planted by first-century Christians exist today. The local church is not meant to be permanent. In the end, only God's kingdom lasts. If in the end our isolationism produces only empty fortresses, what good has been done? Jesus said, "Do not store up for yourselves treasures upon earth, where moth and rust destroy, and where thieves break in and steal. But store up for yourselves treasures in heaven."[6]

Emerging Issue: Leadership Role Shifts

In times of great change, such as the days we live in now, new kinds of leaders surface. They have a different kind of relationship with their culture. In their book *Understanding Folk Religion*, Hiebert, Shaw, and Tienow claim that stable eras of history are characterized by formal religious institutions led by priestly types.

Unstable times breed anti-institutionalism, during which more prophetic types surface and lead.

Priests are leaders in the religious establishment. They represent the people to God and sustain the life of their religious community by exercising ritual and symbolic authority. They get their authority and power from their office, which they acquire through institutional processes such as appointment, election, and inheritance. They are often trained in schools and have mastered the performance of religious rituals. They focus on proper procedures, doing things in an orderly manner, keeping the laws, and following the rules. They are keepers of tradition and corporate memory.[7]

This has been the modern era's leadership paradigm, but the times are changing and we see a shift occurring. Prophets are found "when old structures are inadequate for new situations; times of social turbulence, political turmoil, and spiritual crisis."[8] Prophets of old lived simple and frugal lives,[9] and in the anti-institutional climate of today people are looking for leaders who live more simply. Rather than appointment to an office, prophets gain their authority through their charisma and spiritual credibility, from character and a message of foretelling the truth and exhorting people to focus on God.[10] They tend to self-identify and live in relationship to society and its institutions as outsiders (priests are insiders). In relation to the church, they act as reformers and critics and are detached, with no territorial ties and no place in the hierarchy. They are dynamic change agents,[11] and consequently they are looked at as dangerous opponents of the institutions. The shift of power to leaders of this kind is usually quite threatening to the priestly leaders of modern institutions, but we are nevertheless anticipating the change and the design implications it suggests.

9

A PALETTE OF MODELS

*Two things that in my opinion reinforce one another
and remain eternally true are: Do not quench your
inspiration and your imagination, do not become the
slave of your model; and again: Take the model and
study it, otherwise your inspiration will never become
plastically concrete.*
—VINCENT VAN GOGH[1]

VINCENT VAN GOGH BEGAN HIS CAREER not as an artist but as a
missionary to Belgian coal miners. Sensing that God had called
him to care for the poor, he slept on the floor and gave almost all
his possessions to the miners. Within two years, the Evangelization
Council of the Dutch Reformed Church concluded that although
van Gogh was successful as a minister, his level of zeal was scan-
dalous, so they fired him. The next year, he entered art school at
the Royal Academy in Antwerp, Belgium. Though already painting professionally, he was placed in a beginner's class. Another
student later described a scene at the school: "Van Gogh started
painting feverishly, furiously, with a rapidity that stupefied his fellow students. He laid on his paint so thickly that his colors literally
dripped from his canvas on to the floor."[2] Because of his unruly
style, van Gogh was quickly dismissed from the school.

Van Gogh, one of history's most brilliant artists, was passionate,
unconventional, and experimental. When he learned to paint, however, he first taught himself all of the techniques of every classic artist he possibly could. His artistic breakthroughs were partly a result
of his creative genius, and partially a result of intentional discipline.

We ask you to engage this chapter in a similar way, first by considering a few of the many existing approaches to church structure, and then by applying your own vivid imagination to the process. As we explain various church models, we invite you to consider them as a palette of colors. There are a few primary and secondary colors to consider, but there are also many ways of combining colors, creating hues, and working with contrast to arrive at whole new colors and perceptions of color. Just as some colors are more intense than others, evoke different emotions, or appear to create balance or harmony, we anticipate your experience with church models will do the same.

Church Organizing Principles

Ask a church pastor or planter: "What kind of church do you lead?" or "What kind of church are you starting?" The response will almost certainly be an indicator of the church's organizing principle: some central idea around which a church will focus its attention and answer all its primary questions. Sometimes, the organizing principle is indicated by the name of the church. Church of the Nations, for example, may indicate a missional organizing principle. Usually the organizing principle is cultural (a church for my generation), geographical (a church that reaches this multihousing community), theological (a disciple-making church), denominational (a Methodist Church), or model-driven (a seeker-driven church). Sometimes, the organizing principle includes more than one category (a Baptist seeker-driven church that reaches young African Americans living in this new housing development).

Over the last several decades, descriptors like these have become less and less tidy, transcending categories because church leaders are already designing, refining, and re-aligning, even if they don't realize it. Combining these elements is like mixing colors in new ways to form an extended palette. Some of these new shades of church are interesting and a great complement for where and how the color will be applied, but some are simply not a match. For example, Linda remembers attempting to fashion a creative worship experience for an emotionally hurting creative subculture, but they had the good sense to tell her that in the midst of their pain they needed the steady consistency of a consistent order of liturgy, rather than the mercurial creativity she had tried to put in place through serendipitous worship activities. On the other hand, some experimental mixtures are surprising at first but make sense over time. Reclamation of liturgical-type churches among younger adults, for example, became unexpectedly popular, but it made sense in light of the generation's reaction to the pragmatism of the modern era and how that generation is open to leaning into mystery, rather than the objectivity of the modern scientific methods of dualism and foundationalism.

Colors on the Palette

You are almost at the place in this book where you will begin to make some serious design decisions. In the same way that van Gogh taught himself the techniques of many classic artists before choosing his own artistic style, it is important for you to think clearly about a few church models. As you read, consider the topics raised in previous chapters: your self, your team, your micro- and macrocommunity, your theology and ecclesiology, and the distinctive characteristics of your culture or worldview. As you progress in this chapter, remember everything you articulated about your values, beliefs, and realities. Ask yourself honest questions about how this palette of church models lines up with what you are already thinking about and how you are sensing that God is leading you.

Models, Labels, and Other Confusing Terms

It is difficult to know how to categorize common church models in a way that is both fair and accessible for our readers. People have made many attempts at classification systems, but the act of labeling seems to create division, which is not our intent. At the same time, there are valid similarities and differences between types that make this a worthy, although challenging, task.

When critics compare church models, they often hold their features side by side as if they are comparing Granny Smith apples with Fujis. Usually they are not; they are comparing very different things. For example, it is difficult to compare a "simple church" with a megachurch because the word *simple* is a measure of complexity and the prefix *mega* is a measure of size. Attractional churches are not the opposite of simple churches either. "Attractional" describes the church's gathering mechanism, not its size or complexity. To say that a church is either simple or complex, or small or large, also polarizes options because they are just measures of scale. We have been guilty of comparing apples to oranges, rather than apples to apples in the several models, and in so doing one of the "fruits" pales in the comparison depending on the preference of the person making the observations. Failure to line up similar characteristics actually reduces potential options instead of releasing them.

It makes more sense to ask questions such as: How simple or how complex a structure is needed to serve specific mission, values, and leadership agendas? What size, from mini to mega, functions best within the framework? What range of organizational metaphors will be used ("organic" or mechanistic, or some other)? Some structural issues are actually best expressed as antonyms. For example, a church ecclesiology might be expressed either in the gathering (relational or inwardness, or both) of the local church or in a kingdom perspective (missional with a global parameter), as explained in several previous chapters.

The classification tool we have selected for the purpose of exploring the model colors on the palette is related to gathering principles. We do this cautiously, because we actually do not believe that church exists only when it is gathered. Rather, we approach a discussion of models this way because most new models we know have arisen from the church planting focus of the last half century. Church planters are naturally interested in how to gather people, and they invent new ways to do it. This means there are now many ways to describe churches that developed out of gathering approaches. This is not the same as saying that Bergquist and Karr classify churches by their gathering principle; we absolutely do not. The classifications here are simply descriptive tools to assist our readers in discovering preferences and distinctions in their designing, refining, and re-aligning decisions. Three ways of gathering people serve our purposes: attractional, relational, and legacy.

Attractional

The primary gathering strategy of attractional-type churches is to invite people from the community into some widely publicized front door of the church. A lot of time, energy, and financial resources are spent answering the question, "How do we bring people in, and how do we keep them here?" Healthy attractional churches gather large numbers of people because of their evangelistic priority, and not merely with the goal of building a large organization. Attractional methodologies include things like offering high-quality worship service formats (professional-quality music, video, and entertaining communication), hosting large community events and programs that are based on a community's felt needs, and using advertising strategies such as mailing pieces, Internet blitzes, and phone campaigns.

Relational

Relational approaches to church connect and gather people primarily through personal relationships. People in churches of this model focus on people whom they know, meet, or can invite face-to-face. The healthiest relational churches do not gather people out of a reaction to more traditionally structured kinds of churches. Nor do they gather people merely out of a craving for authentic community. The newest, healthiest relational churches gather as communitas around missional and incarnational purposes, including community service or a social meal that can be combined with other biblical activities of the church.

Legacy

Legacy models draw newcomers from the outside to the inside of their church by virtue of legitimacy, reputation, or some comfort bridge. Instead of churches proactively finding people, people find them. Some legacy models are neighborhood churches where Christians who are looking for a nearby parish find comfort in attending whichever church is closest, thus choosing to make an investment in their community. Some people choose legacy models because of their heritage in a "name-brand" denomination or customary style of worship. People who need churches that reflect their language or culture look for a match. Legacy churches gather people without even trying, simply because of who they are.

Characteristics of Attractional Churches

Attractional-model churches usually have seven characteristics in common:

1. The front door of the church (the means by which people are introduced to the church) is almost always some kind of central gathering, while assimilation and discipleship happen in a smaller group.
2. These churches are centrally and usually hierarchically organized for efficient decision making. Strong organizational leadership skills and work styles are demanded.
3. Everyone knows that first impressions matter, so much attention is given to the many details of a qualitative "user experience." This includes but is not limited to impressive preaching, music, and children's ministry.
4. The meeting place for the church matters. It must be geographically accessible, physically presentable (even commendable), and large enough for continued growth.
5. Multiple ministries to the community are outwardly focused and based on community needs and interests.
6. They usually define some sociologically homogeneous population group as a "target community."
7. Most successful seeker churches use some kind of advertising approach. In general, the message is "come, hear, see, and experience."

Common Attractional Church Models

Seeker Churches

Churches that identify themselves as seekers design around the theological priority of evangelism. Other aspects of church life such as worship and fellowship usually submit to evangelism, a factor that is particularly evident in large gatherings. This model is based on an assumption that many people are genuinely interested in spirituality and are therefore somewhere on a spiritual pilgrimage that will lead them eventually to the Christian faith. These churches work to make a place available for those who are seeking help with their spiritual journey. They aim to eliminate as many barriers to the gospel as possible by creating a low-commitment, nonthreatening "come as you are" environment.

The two best-known seeker-style churches are known as "seeker sensitive" (geared toward people in various stages of Christian pilgrimage) and "seeker driven" (focusing almost all of their energy on people who are not Christians). The main gathering event of the seeker-driven church is not intended to be a worship service, but rather an entertaining introduction to the faith, because seekers are presumably not ready to worship a God they don't know. Sometimes these churches offer additional services for people who are already followers of Jesus and want to worship.

In contrast, seeker-sensitive churches offer some kind of user-friendly worship service, adapting the number of songs, the style of music, and the lyrics for the seekers among them. Seeker-sensitive churches also differ among themselves as they adapt to macrocultures that are friendly, ambivalent, or hostile to Christianity.

Purpose-Driven Churches

Purpose-driven churches take their name from a model developed by Rick Warren, founder of Saddleback Church in Southern California. This model of attractional church differs from seeker churches, even though the typical worship services of both may seem quite similar. True purpose-driven churches are driven by the five primary purposes of the church as identified by Warren: worship, discipleship, ministry, mission, and fellowship. At Saddleback, these purposes are held together, with each encoded in every sphere of church life (staffing, programming, budgeting, and resource management). The five purposes are championed by leaders with ministry calling in an arena.

Multisite (Team and Satellite)

Theoretically, a multisite church, or a church that meets in many locations, could embrace any kind of church structure or model. However, the primary multisite models operate more like a collective of seeker or purpose-driven churches. The same teaching pastor often speaks in each location at a different time or by satellite, although this is certainly not always the case. Many multisite churches have discovered through trial and error that attempting to broadcast video to other campuses during the music elements or times of prayer is largely unsuccessful. Instead, in an attempt to build a solid sense of community and connection, most multisite churches produce music, worship, and prayer at each satellite campus. Additionally, these times help create a unique environment, distinct from that of the main campus, while remaining true to the brand and identity of the church.

Because of technology, multisite churches are geographically less restricted. Each site shares values and vision, as well as practical things such as a budget and staff. Once established, churches and sites sometimes use name recognition as an advertising technique, leveraging the good reputation of the brand of the church or the fame of the pastor, or both.

There are many other kinds of churches that use attractional gathering methodologies. Some focus on bringing Christians through their doors. They use everything from large events to large phone book advertisements to attract congregants. Linda remembers a San Diego church that amped up its Sunday evening services at the exact time that other local churches abandoned theirs. The church brought in notable Christian speakers and musicians who attracted Christians accustomed to attending church twice on Sundays. As a result, the church grew to a large size, primarily because of its new capacity to attract and draw Christians from other churches.

Strengths and Opportunities of Attractional Churches

Attractional churches have been some of the fastest-growing in America for several decades. They have attracted many new people to the Christian faith because they take evangelism seriously. They work especially well in homogeneous communities that are already well seeded with the gospel. They also work well in cultures that are still influenced strongly by modernism and in which centralized organizational systems are still perceived as the best way to organize. Because of their potential size, and large budgets, they have a great opportunity to influence their communities. Many now embrace starting new churches and have become sending bases for likeminded new churches. They use mechanisms such as advertising to help them quickly sift through thousands of potential new church members that it might take years to connect with in some other way.

Weaknesses and Challenges of Attractional Churches

It takes a lot of money to start, lead, run, and reproduce an attractional church. Although this is changing, the high investment of resources required to sustain the organization means many of these churches never develop a kingdom ecclesiology. Relatively few people have the necessary gifts and abilities required to lead this kind of church. Unless an individual finds his or her way into a small group, assimilation can be difficult. As a result, there can be a large back door. Pastors and congregants may never know one another; people can come and go without ever forging a meaningful relationship. There are other challenges for churches with the most radical seeker commitments. How will worship happen for those who already know God? To what extent is the gospel able to be contextualized but not trivialized? How and where will newcomers to the faith grow spiritually?

What It Takes (Optimally)
- *Self.* A multigifted, visionary leader with great communication skills, a huge time commitment, entrepreneurial leadership style, good group dynamic ability, either missionary gifts or relevance (indigenous or learned over time) to the community, the capacity to draw others around a vision or help others discover a shared vision; and if married, complete spousal commitment.
- *Team.* A gifted, committed core group, including talented musicians, children's workers, administrative help, technicians, and group leaders, either missionary gifts or relevance (indigenous or learned over time) to the community. The more diverse and committed the team, the less there is for the pastor to be responsible for alone.
- *Ecclesiology/theology.* Commitment to evangelism, willingness to contextualize scripture, comfort level with more hierarchical ecclesial organizations, comfort with the belief that people are seeking God (and not just God seeking people).

- *Macrocommunity.* A community that is already seeded with the gospel (or willingness for the team to take the time to seed the community), is open to the gospel, does not carry excess baggage about the church and is willing to gather for religious purposes, a more consumer or audience culture (as opposed to a participatory culture), a culture where people have been exposed to the gospel though many do not yet attend church.
- *Practical considerations.* A lot of money for advertising, equipment, and more, plus a level of comfort spending money on these things; a large, appropriate meeting space available at a time when people are willing to meet, a place to park or good public transportation nearby, adequate pastoral salary so that the pastor can focus on beginning the church rather than on fundraising or other supplementary employment.

Characteristics of Relational Churches

Churches that attract people relationally usually have seven traits in common:

1. They tend to be structured simply and are organized as either a single cell or a decentralized network of affiliated cell groups.
2. They may be lay or bivocationally led, but generally they have less of a clergy-lay distinction because leadership is based more on spiritual and relational authority than on positional authority structures.
3. They are structured to reproduce very quickly because they need very little money, have no real space considerations, and can use almost any willing Christian as a leader.
4. They not only gather relationally but also focus both internally (ministry to one another) and externally (evangelism and hospitality) on relationship. Intimacy and accountability are byproducts.
5. Gatherings are informal and participatory. They tend to emphasize many spiritual gifts (not just one, such as teaching, over others such as hospitality, evangelism, or service).
6. They can meet anywhere at anytime: homes, restaurants, or ministry centers.

7. The church as described in Acts Chapter 2 is core to relational church ecclesiology.

Common Relational Church Models

House Churches/Simple Churches

These churches are basic Christian communities that form relationally around a simple way of life and mission. There are several kinds of simple churches, which differ from one another most distinctly in how they balance the values of communal life and missional life. Some begin as Christians gathering in communities because they prefer more intimate, simpler ways of being a church. Sometimes they share a mutual dissatisfaction with traditionally structured churches. They see themselves as some day reproducing, but most never do.

Other types of simple churches, such as what is called the "organic church" movement, begin out of relationships formed with people who are not Christians and then spread to the natural (organic) relationships of those people. Leaders for new generations of churches come from those previously non-Christian peoples. These congregations are relational in nature, but the intimacy they share is born out of a common mission and common proclamation of the Lordship of Christ. It is increasingly common for these organic churches to form loose decentralized networks for fellowship, accountability, mission, and training; examples are forming in almost every large city.

The former kind of simple church is oriented more toward community than mission (come and experience community), while the latter is oriented more toward mission than community (go and tell or show Jesus to others). Worship works itself out differently too. Some simple churches worship the same as their traditional church counterparts; for others incarnational ministry is in itself a way of worship (Rom. 12:1–2).

Intentional Christian Communities

This term refers to followers of Jesus who live together in one house or some other close living situation such as a farm, an apartment complex, or a neighborhood. Close personal proximity exaggerates the need for the relational aspect of these churches to work well. Where intentional communities succeed, it is usually because of positive relational dynamics and a common set of values. When they implode, it is because of negative relational dynamics and a lack of shared values. Intentional communities range from high- to low-structure and accountability, and they may choose to meet only with one another, take their common life into a larger community, or invite a larger community to join them in mission. Some choose where the community will live together on the basis of mission.

Cell Churches

We identify cell churches as relational because in a true cell church the small relational community is where most of the life of the church takes place. The organizing principle is that the basic Christian unit of fellowship, spiritual growth, and evangelism happens at the cellular level. They grow by reproducing leaders who begin new cells. Cells usually meet periodically for joint worship or common mission. Cell churches are hybrid models in that they can be expensive, be centralized, use paid staff, and sometimes own and maintain buildings.

Strengths and Opportunities of Relational Churches

Most kinds of relational churches require little money because their primary currency is relationship. They can meet anywhere (homes, restaurants, community centers) and at any time. It is easier to gather a few people at flexible times through relationships (for example, nurses who work the night shift in a hospital). Leadership requirements are spiritual and relational and require no formal training or special abilities. With the exception of cell churches and some incarnational ministry models where people may be paid for running a nonprofit, leaders do not usually receive a salary. For all of these reasons, relational churches are largely reproducible. In addition, because money is not used for buildings or salaries, they are potentially able to invest more in outside causes. Most relational models are highly participatory, and so they do not require as much time from only one leader, thereby offering a more leisurely lifestyle for all involved. They can be adapted easily in many cultural contexts, including those opposing Christianity. Examples are *mnemone* (Afghans) and *satsang* (East Indian), both practices in the San Francisco Bay Area context and cultural adaptations of spiritual focus that have worked successfully. Because they are relationally driven, there is a high level of member accountability.

Weaknesses and Challenges of Relational Churches

Relational churches need to stay focused on embracing missional DNA and not default to a practice of only relational DNA. Single churches, not related to the larger body of Christ, easily lose sight of mission and become ingrown. Many relational churches work so hard at the group community aspect of church that they never get around to evangelism or mission. Some relational churches seem to attract unhealthy people, including those who were disgruntled in traditional churches, high-maintenance people, and those choosing smaller fellowships to feel like big fish in a small pond. One criticism, which Allan and Linda have not personally experienced in relational churches, is that there is a higher potential for heresy. The fear of heresy persists from those in other models despite the greater degree of accountability addressed by emerging church networks. Another challenge comes from outside this model: relational churches are often undervalued by leaders of nonrelational ones because they are less focused on measuring success by numbers and more focused on measuring it in relationship to personal and community transformation. This matters only for relational churches wishing to be accepted in a denomination, or seen as valid by the other churches in their community for cooperative purposes.

What It Takes (and What It Doesn't Take)
- *Self.* Almost anyone who knows and appropriately loves himself or herself, knows and loves God, and knows and loves people can plant some kind of church through relationships. Planting, leading, and nurturing this kind of church community takes no formal training, but it does require mentoring relationships. Leaders must also embrace an intentional kingdom-oriented lifestyle, an outward focus, and an incarnational view toward holistic community transformation.

- *Team.* Anyone who cannot draw together a team of some kind may not be relationally adept at leading a relational church. Relationships within the team ought to be strong and clear enough that team members can spend more time engaged in mission and less time trying to figure out how to relate.
- *Ecclesiology.* A strong belief in the gifts and callings of God's people is critical. To plant healthy, reproducing, incarnational churches, the church community needs to share a commitment to mission as an organizing principle and a way of life. Leadership is understood relationally, spiritually, and as gift-based rather than hierarchical.
- *Practical considerations.* This way of being a church requires very little money, primarily because it does not entail having a building, and because in most situations leaders should expect to receive income from a source other than the church. Receiving blessing from denominations and local churches as support may be difficult in many situations, until this model is more widely accepted.

Characteristics of Legacy Models

Legacy churches generally have these six things in common:

1. By definition, they connect the past and the present, and though they are positioned well to address the future most have not yet imagined how their model could be uniquely positioned to transform their changing macrocommunity.
2. For the same reasons, they are generally bound to more traditional approaches, including traditional programs, worship services, and methodologies for structure and decision making.
3. Most are slower to embrace change because they either build or inherit a set of cultural expectations from their organization.
4. The source of their legitimacy is often also their organizing principle, for example, a First Baptist Church that makes the decisions, offers programs, and purchases resources from what is offered or preferred by its denomination, and inherits legitimacy among those looking to be members in a Baptist church.

5. They usually own a church building, because it is part of their legitimacy. People find them partly because the building is there.
6. Attractional churches that grow very large may become legacy churches over the years. These churches stop needing to find people because so many people find them.

Common Legacy Church Models

Denominational Churches

Committed Catholics look for Catholic churches and their Lutheran counterparts look for Lutheran churches. This may be true even for people who disagree with some major practices or tenets of their faith. Denominational legacy models are organized in light of denominational expectations, doctrines, creeds, practices, and traditions that have served the denomination well. For example, when Linda's parents move to a new city they almost always check out a local Methodist church before trying any others. That's who they are: Methodists.

Models Based on Worship Style

Some people are attracted to a church because they are accustomed to the style of worship or liturgy. Don't change how communion is practiced, and don't offer them a French Taizé service. Use the hymnody with which they have become familiar, pronounce the Lord's Prayer on a weekly basis, and they feel at home. Pentecostal Christians want to be part of Pentecostal congregations, and if there are none within forty miles they may pass by many other congregations to find a community of practice where they can be nurtured and enriched according to a familiar worship encounter.

Neighborhood Churches

Some people prefer church communities near home. They may want the convenience of a nearby church, they may want to connect better with their neighbors, and some may long for the holism afforded by proximity to live as a family, work, and be part of schools and churches that are embedded within their own neighborhood. The neighborhood church with a pleasing exterior, a full parking lot on Sunday morning, some weekday presence (such as a preschool or a midweek program), and its name being a household word can and does draw congregants on the basis of a community reputation.

A hybrid version of the neighborhood legacy model is the geographically indigenous unit, where churches meet in a defined setting such as a mobile home park, apartment complex, nursing home, dormitory, or residential hotel, and people define their natural microcommunity as those living within this boundary. The most natural, organic way for leaders to design an autonomous church is within those microcommunities. The organizing principle is similar to the relational models such as house church, but with a narrowly defined geographic microcommunity strategy. People choose these churches for many of the same reasons they choose other neighborhood churches.

Strengths and Opportunities of Legacy Churches

Legacy churches have the opportunity to influence the future by offering wisdom, relationship, financial resources, and property to new churches. They can be intentionally generative and continuously reproducing. Linda remembers a church she visited in Arizona that classified itself as a traditional church filled with senior adults. The church was positioned in the middle of an expansive retirement community and was a completely indigenous, missionally focused church. It had a bright and beautiful worship facility and incorporated all the latest technology. Linda challenged the church to embrace a new image of itself; instead of a traditional church, they were in fact a legacy church poised to usher in the future for new generations of retirees. Legacy churches are also loyal to their roots. This can make them less subject to certain kinds of heresy because they do not feel a need to create outside of what already exists, and legacy churches are affirmed by their denomination.

Weaknesses and Challenges of Relational Churches

Younger generations tend to abandon or ignore legacy churches in favor of creating new kinds of church paradigms. Because legacy churches are bound by some traditions, new ideas can be suspect.

Many have not even considered how much potential they have to influence the future; instead they adopt a maintenance posture. Many of the challenges of attractional churches are inherent in the legacy model; in addition to the positive legacy that can spring from a rich history, these churches can also carry baggage (insular microcultures, cliques, control mechanisms, and white elephants, as in everyone in leadership being related).

What It Takes
The legacy model requires an appreciation of historical context, a love and appreciation for tradition, or a desire to be embedded in a community. In the neighborhood model, leadership looks more like a parish priest than a businessperson or expedition leader. Denominational models require loyalty and trust from participants, similar to how large families are committed to sticking together even when the denomination is wrong or experiencing strife. This commitment is true even when some members of the family are dysfunctional. We anticipate a brave new kind of legacy model taking shape on the horizon that will be based on a younger generation's need for roots and holistic community transformation.

Experimenting with Models: Allan's Story

This story describes how Allan and his team worked to find the kind of church that best fit what God was calling them to start. Just as in the Lewis and Clark story with which this book started, there were no maps, only a journey of discovery. We use some of the same design elements addressed throughout this book to tell their story.

Self

Allan values close relationships. He prefers simply structured organizations and dislikes bureaucracy. He is missional and wired for the future, but he also lives well in the present tense with practical applications of experimental ideas. He makes room in his life to care for his family, friends, and community. Allan works full-time, so his free time is limited.

Team

Allan and his wife, Kathy, enjoy working together as ministry partners. As parents, they want their children to be active in mission and ministry as a normal way of life, and they also love investing in other young leaders from diverse cultural backgrounds. Their home is always filled with ministry-oriented young people. The whole team (family and core group) values multicultural relationships and holds a vision for a ministry that embraces many peoples.

Macrocommunity

The Karrs' home is located in the Denver metro area, where many cultures and backgrounds are represented. The people groups in the metro area include (among many others) Karen, Hispanic, Mongolian, Romanian, Bhutanese, Pakistani, and Zambian. Many subcultures are also present, from cowboys to bikers.

Theology or Ecclesiology

Allan and his team envision holistic community transformation and accessibility to God's love for all people. Their imagination for church is fired by the church in the book of Acts, and by what they know about church planting movements overseas. They are convicted that Jesus' way is to go and tell rather than come and hear or experience. They believe in wise stewardship of money, which means they prefer low-budget ways of organizing churches.

Practical Considerations

The Karr family owns a nice home, and they are willing to use it for ministry. Allan and Kathy's full-time jobs mean that the time they have for other ministries is limited. Not much money is available to fund church starting, but they know people who are willing to invest in the vision even without being paid.

Synthesis

Relational models suit the family and core team best, but they are also invested in a kingdom theology. They desire both intimacy and mission—the small house church and a way to make a difference in the metro area. Leaders from many cultures have sought Allan as their mentor, and some of them follow attractional or legacy gathering practices. From his missional and relational influences, Allan led his own simple church to form a network of eighteen churches to date that includes every one of the Denver metro cultures and subcultures listed earlier. His team's sense of simplicity and intimacy helped them conceptualize this network relationally rather than institutionally. The model that emerged out of these values is now called the Protean Model.

The Protean Model

Allan and his team began their church in a home. They had a vision for a network of autonomous but relationally connected churches that was multicultural, multiethnic, and international in scope and mission. Structurally they imagined something that functioned like one body with many parts. They called it Ethne Church Network, taken from the phrase panta ta ethne. Furthermore, they dreamed of a church network that was not simply engaged in worship but more important would be active in its community. Members would all be encouraged and supported in missionally focused lifestyles.

A couple of years after it began, Ethne started reproducing churches that looked very different from one another in form, style, language, and culture. None of the church models that were already on the palette were sufficient to explain or contain the newly emerging Ethne, so Allan and other leaders worked together to find a way to help the network release its potential. Finding form was difficult; no one church expression represented the whole. The picture that sprang to life reminded them of the mythological story of Proteus, the Greek god who altered his physical form (shape shifting) according to the situation or encounter. They decided to call the model of Ethne Church Network the Protean model.[3]

A values-based DNA began to emerge within the network. The originating church that Allan and his team founded carried all of the values of the Ethne mother church. But just as human offspring are not identical clones of either parent, the DNA shows up in varying degrees in all of Ethne's eighteen congregations at this time. Ethne values and is committed to seeing and living out holistic community transformation, being flexible enough to morph as quickly as needed, structuring simply, promoting group participation with a value of cooperation, and being positioned to be missional among all peoples.

Over time, Ethne sponsored and adopted churches that embodied attractional, relational, and legacy models. The Ethne network became known for valuing and empowering all peoples, and not trying to control its member churches. All of the Ethne congregations are eager to participate in cooperative network endeavors. For example, the first-generation Romanian congregation assisted at and catered a celebration for a new English-speaking traditional church comprising older Caucasians. A Ukrainian congregation also helped by bringing food. Ethne Church Network[4] started as a house church, but it morphed over time and, led by the Spirit of God, created something that was even more than the initial core team ever hoped or imagined.

10

DISCOVERING CONGRUENCY

*When I start a picture, I always have a script, but
I change it every day, I put in what occurs to me that
day, out of my imagination. You start on a voyage;
you know where you will end up, but not what will
occur along the way. You want to be surprised.*
—FEDERICO FELLINI[1]

RIGHT IN THE MIDDLE of the Bergquists' backyard is a seventy-
five-year-old camellia tree. It takes up so much room and its
branches give so much shade that a sizeable portion of the yard
is configured around it. If they were designing from scratch, the
Bergquists would never have introduced the camellia tree as
the yard's dominant feature, but they value the lovely old tree and
respect its presence. Eric's design solution was to prune the tree
upward in such a way that its branches are now high enough for
them to plant under and around it.

Many of you are in the same situation. There is something
about your church or community context that you need to prune
or work around in order to respect both the old and the new,
what God is doing now, and what God put in place in another era.
Perhaps the tree in the middle of the yard is your own irregular,
bivocational work schedule, a deacon who wields too much power,
a local regulation banning churches that meet in homes, an urban
neighborhood with no parking, a musty old building you wish you
could sell, a gated community you wish you could penetrate, a bird
sanctuary that was discovered on the land you purchased, a tacky
mural painted by the church's oldest saint, a venerated pulpit, a

canonized hymnbook, the customary passing of the plate, or the traditional passing of the peace. All of these things can present the opportunity for a reality check that points to the need for pruning, reshaping, and reconfiguring. It's what church refiners and re-aligners do, but even designers never completely escape the process. What do you need to landscape around, and how will you do it with integrity and grace?

There are other aspects of the Bergquists' property that make gardening a challenge. Because it is in the middle of a fog belt, plants that require full sun, such as roses and tomatoes, are difficult to grow. Their home is located close to a golf course and other open spaces that have attracted a healthy subterranean gopher community. The rodents swiftly consume their own favorite plants, which happen to be some of the Bergquists' favorite plants too. The gopher population can be annoying, but it contributes to the biodiversity of the neighborhood, even attracting beautiful red-tailed hawks. Communitywide use of poison to oust the gophers is not an option, so Eric simply elevates certain plants in large pots and puts wire mesh baskets around others.

The Bergquists' backyard is designed around values (the tree and the gophers) and practical realities (the fog and the gophers), similar to how we will ask you to think through the issues in this chapter. There will be things about yourself, your team, your culture, or your church situation that you wish you could change but cannot alter. In this chapter we are looking for congruency: design elements that are in agreement with, suitable for, and appropriate to each other and to what God is calling you into.

Values Congruency for Churches

Although the Bergquists have learned to live well with the existing features of their backyard, they are still able to make many gardening and landscaping decisions. One of the lessons they have learned is to sort through the categories and species of plants and prioritize the many defining elements of each in order to find the right plants that fit the various criteria of their yard. For example, they choose some plants on the basis of a personal value of sustainability and creation care by selecting from many drought-tolerant species. They select other plants that are classified as shade, partial shade, or partial sun varieties, from the reality of the San Francisco weather. There are all kinds of personal preferences to consider, such as color, size, texture, and shape. Some plants are in the yard just because the Bergquists enjoy them; no explanation is needed. As a church designer, refiner, or re-aligner, you will also make many decisions, some of which include sorting to meet your criteria. As you do, you will make many other kinds of decisions too. The process will cause you to consider how those choices work together to form a harmonious picture of what God is asking of you.

Congruency Around Your Big Idea

In Chapter Nine, we classified churches in only one way, by the gathering mechanism—attractional, relational, or legacy. Here are three tables (10.1, 10.2, 10.3) to illustrate these categories.

Now, we are asking you to lay those categories aside. Just as plants can be classified by many features, the same practice may be applied to churches. They can be evaluated as urban, suburban, or rural parishes; contemporary, traditional, postmodern, or charismatic worship styles; Catholic, Episcopal, or Presbyterian affiliation; and more. One good way to think about churches is by organizing principle—your big idea. In Chapter Nine we said that church organizing principles are usually cultural, theological, denominational, or model-driven. For example, consider how churches use theological organizing principles. It is possible to organize theologically around worship, prayer, community, mission, evangelism, service, the commands of Christ, and so forth.

Other churches organize around vision or mission (the words are often used interchangeably, though they are not the same thing). These two concepts are often conceptualized in ways that align with specific church models. For instance, ministry-based models generally operate with vision and mission statements that are related to biblical themes of justice, reconciliation, and transformation. Some churches, denominations, and church consulting groups approach the concepts of vision and mission the same way profit-making businesses do. It is appropriate for business enterprises to talk about these things in terms of what they visualize, want, or need for their own firms. Nobody calls this selfish

TABLE 10.1. ATTRACTIONAL STRATEGY MODELS.

Model	Organizing Principle	Distinctives	Challenges
Seeker-driven church	Evangelistic priority with a culturally and sociologically defined target group: unchurched non-Christians	Program-based seeker priority in main services, quality is defined culturally, nonconfrontational	Christian growth can be shallow; expensive model; requires exceptional, narrowly gifted leader; depends on seekers
Seeker-sensitive church	Evangelistic priority for unchurched/unbelievers in the context of community of believers	Program-based; markets outreach to community; worship service is front door; churchy language avoided; user-friendly	Also expensive; same challenges as seeker-driven; a new, spiritually aware seeker-type person now in culture
Purpose-driven church	Balance biblical purposes of the church with evangelism to the lost	Program-based and purpose-driven staff, structure, and ministry according to agreed biblical purposes of the church	Reproduction is an expensive model; dangerous reliance on methods and strategies; difficult to balance purposes, so they often yield to evangelism
Affinity-based church	Organized around a particular language, culture, subculture, interest, disability, etc.	Usually program-based; tend to be homogeneous to the organizing principle	Generational sustainability; sometimes so homogeneous it needs diversity
Multicultural church	Diversity and proximity provide the platform for doing life together and being the church	Relational; culturally relevant; value diversity and many cultures; value tolerance	One culture dominates others. potentially expensive; leaders must reflect the values of the neighbor-sphere; may be forced
Multisite satellite church	One church meeting in multiple locations; attractional model where a noted speaker or leader is often the draw at multiple sites	Sophisticated use of technology, geographically unrestricted, brand name marketing, common use of video venues, shared resources	Impersonal, undiscipled church members, difficulty in relationship connections

TABLE 10.2. RELATIONAL STRATEGY MODELS.

Model	Organizing Principle	Distinctives	Challenges
House church, simple church	Biblical Christianity in microcommunity as a way of life and mission	Simple in structure, do not meet in church buildings; lower operating budget; mobile, informal, and make decisions quickly, led bivocationally	Can become inwardly focused; child care is often problematic; criticized by institutions and denominations
Intentional Christian communities	The church is expressed by communal living and missional principles	Usually in a focused living arrangement; high value for microcommunity, discipleship	Can become inwardly focused; living with others can cause disunity
Cell churches	Basic Christian unit of fellowship, spiritual growth, and evangelism is the cell community, but there is also a larger gathering	Reproducing cells, life in microcommunity; cells linked together as part of a larger church with strong focus of authority	Sometimes cell is undermined by controlling leadership; cell becomes inwardly focused or perceived to be
Relationally based church networks	Biblical Christianity in microcommunities that network with each other as a way of life and mission	Decentralized leadership, network churches are often autonomous, and can include a variety of structures; relational, accountability among churches	Reproduction can be messy; organization is too loose for some preferences

TABLE 10.3. LEGACY STRATEGY MODELS.

Model	Organizing Principle	Distinctives	Challenges
Denominational church	Usually fashioned around a denominational framework of expectations	Program-based schedule and front door; institutionally structured for leadership and decisions	Target is aging; expensive buildings, programs, and staffing; can become inwardly focused
Worship style, liturgical church	Designed around an accustomed style, worship, art, or liturgy	Comfort afforded by beauty, familiarity, and heritage, renewed liturgical models now available, often associated as mainline	Usually expensive; limited by traditions; change is difficult
Neighbor-sphere church	Built around spheres of relationships, usually geographically close	Microcommunity-oriented; usually geographically defined; committed to the mission of the people in their neighbor-sphere; often multicultural	Will likely never be mega in scope; tolerance for all cultures in the neighbor-sphere
Geographic indigenous unit church	Church is formed in a narrowly defined geographic microcommunity	Mobile home parks, multifamily housing, nursing homes, dorms, etc., form autonomous church	Sustainability, leadership; training needed; seasonal or short-lived

or introspective because most for-profit businesses exist for the purpose of something that benefits the corporation and helps it make money. For example, Starbucks's mission statement for its employees is to "establish Starbucks as the premier purveyor of the finest coffee in the world while maintaining our uncompromising principles as we grow."[2] The terms of this statement would be completely inappropriate for a church.

Here are some real-life vision statements from churches that care deeply about their members, and even their immediate neighborhood, but fail to embrace God's global vision.

. . . to be a church where you can SEE Christ.

To be a family of all ages, colors, languages, backgrounds, and tax brackets, united by and growing through our faith in and love for Jesus. To be citizens of the kingdom of God who go out with Jesus daily, to show His love in word and deed to whomever God chooses to bring our way.

We are committed to be a loving church, spiritually nurturing to ourselves and the community, by living and serving enthusiastically in our faith in Jesus Christ. We are a church of prayer and mission.

When they base their vision and mission on the inward needs and desires of their own organization, as in these examples, churches do not position themselves to embrace a more biblical, missional kingdom vision. They never intended to structure themselves in a way that hindered their embracing God's global priorities, but it happened. A church that says it is kingdom-oriented but organizes around something that suggests otherwise eventually experiences values incongruence. For example, it is wonderful for a church to want to "see" Jesus, but to carry out its mission it needs to help other people see Jesus as well. No doubt this church sees itself as mission-minded, but its vision doesn't help it to move in a missional direction. The other vision statements each contain a similar flaw.

Still other churches organize around values. For example, one of the most interesting new Christian movements is called "the New Monasticism." Christians from many streams of faith who are committed to a simple communal way of life and mission embrace a set of shared values. A multidenominational group of transformational Christians came together in 2005 and as a result of their shared community collaborated to write a document called "The Twelve Marks of New Monasticism," which articulates a way of actively engaging the world, relating to other followers of Christ, caring for creation, and supporting individuals and families.[3] The New Monastics are consistent in organizing around their values.

Let's consider some examples of values misalignment that show up in many congregations. If your two-year-old simple church has never reproduced itself and only added other Christians, then there is something about the church that is not consistent with an evangelistic operating principle. If the first step your church makes to tighten its belt in a financial crisis is to withdraw neighborhood service programs, perhaps it is not as organized around community transformation as you imagine. When your "missional" church promotes a missional lifestyle but expects a level of involvement that requires more than ten hours a week attending church activities and serving other church members, what message is it sending? What needs re-alignment to be organized around your actual beliefs? Are there core values of your church that are more consistent with good business practices than with the practice of obeying Christ? If you are designing from scratch, what is the organizing principle around which you will structure, and how will that be championed? Does the organizing principle, whether it is based on theology, model and vision, culture, or something else, align with what the congregation really values and believes? Which of the church models presented best line up with what you already believe? Which structures or models serve rather than dictate the vision or story to which God is calling the church?

Personal and Team Values

Jim Misloski facilitates a church network in northern Colorado. He is also a professional graphic designer, but his approach to church leadership did not allow for his artistic sensibility. After a long period of frustration, Jim finally gave himself permission to re-align his church model so he could both lead the church and honor his passion. Jim and his church are now envisioning a new direction, experimenting with how he could lead a faith community and exercise his artistic passions (he even contributed to this book by helping with the figures).

Earlier in this book, we addressed the topics of self and micro-community. We say again that who you are and what you think, believe, and enjoy are really important. Your personal values affect design decisions in a variety of potential areas, among them feelings, family, and lifestyle. One way we both teach students about church planting is to assign them to visit a variety of churches and ask that they write reports about their experiences. Some students respond emotively: "I'm really not into that kind of preaching (or music, or style) of church. I prefer large churches (small churches). I can't see myself becoming part of a church like that" (or "If only there were a church like that in my town").

Perhaps you have already experienced a reaction to one or more of the church models we presented, and you sense that one makes your heart sing and another causes it to wither. For example, the city that activated your visionizing capacity seems too dense, and living there terrifies you. Listen to God first, but respect your emotions as His gift. Different church models are conducive to certain lifestyles, too; some models are not easily imagined without a busy, driven type of lifestyle and a high degree of intentionality, while others call for a slower pace with more time dedicated to personal relationships. Some church models are more appropriate than others for your family's chosen way of life.

Consider how you feel about various church experiences, and about the life you believe you were created to live. Which seem most consistent with your personal and family goals and how God has been forming you? How might some models compromise your values while others help you realize them? Is God asking you to adapt to a new way of life, or are you preoccupied with a popular church model that is asking you to make changes incongruent with whom you are created to be? How much change is possible, given your current situation?

Practical Congruency

The Spirit of God is free to ask Christians to follow Him into situations that are not practical, are not culturally acceptable, and make no apparent sense. The Apostle Paul, for example, called himself a fool for Christ. Paul Yonggi-Cho, founder of the Full Gospel Church in Korea, defied culture by obeying God and using women to lead thousands of small groups. God can intervene with all of our strategies and alignment observations any time He chooses, but meanwhile He has also given us resources for discerning practical wisdom. You can prevent heartbreaking mistakes by stopping to check for potential design flaws.

One classic example of a design flaw is the Ford Pinto. When introduced in 1971 as the first Ford subcompact, consumers loved the car because it was small, peppy, and fuel-efficient. The problem? The early Pinto was designed so that its gas tank would rupture very easily, a flaw that caused the vehicle to explode and injure people in many cases. Another example of a serious design flaw resulted in the flooding that occurred in New Orleans in 2005 after hurricane Katrina. The article below appeared in *USA Today*.

Now we want you to consider some common practical considerations that can both prevent design disaster and enhance viability. We include personal, team, relational, financial, cultural, and even timing issues that can ultimately affect important decisions.

RESEARCHERS SAY LEVEES HAD DESIGN FLAWS

NEW ORLEANS (AP) The engineers who designed the floodwalls that collapsed during Hurricane Katrina did not fully consider the porousness of the Louisiana soil or make other calculations that would have pointed to the need for stronger levees with deeper pilings and wider bases, researchers say.

At least one key scenario was ignored in the design, say the researchers, who are scheduled to report their findings at a congressional hearing Wednesday: the possibility that canal water might seep into the dirt on the dry side of the levees, thereby weakening the embankment holding up the floodwalls.

"I'd call it a design omission," said Robert Bea, a University of California at Berkeley civil engineering professor who took part in the study for the National Science Foundation.[4]

Personal Congruency

Church models require their own skill sets, some of which we addressed in Chapter Nine. For example, seeker churches need excellent communicators and excellent musicians. Parish neighborhood churches want compassionate caregivers, and simple churches just need good people who really love God and really love people. Through the years, the two of us have seen many church leaders follow models, realizing much later that the requirements of those models simply did not match their beliefs, values, personalities, abilities, or talents.

One Bay Area church planter tried to start a church in the new Rivermark Community of Santa Clara, California, but he failed miserably. Andy Wood moved into the same community a few years later and launched a new church with more than two hundred people. Why? It would be easy to say that it was because he had a great team, some sacrificial partnering churches, and a large prayer support system, but that would be only part of the story. Why did the first plant fail and the second attempt succeed in this city in the heart of the Silicon Valley? The reason Andy had the ingredients he needed is that he went out after them. He is visionary, vital, entrepreneurial, and a people gatherer. His gifts align appropriately with the dream and the task God gave him to accomplish; this giftedness was missing in the first attempt.

Team Congruency

Andy is not the only gifted, visionary, people gatherer on his team. His wife, Stacie, and two other couples who moved across the country to invest their lives in California's Silicon Valley are a lot like Andy, but with complementary leadership gifts. In another example, Jim Craig, a former school superintendent, became the administrator of Del Cerro Baptist Church in the San Diego area and helped organize the middle-aged church so that it tripled in growth during the decade he served there. Jim wore many hats, but the one that helped the church most was his ability to re-align ministries and programs in a way that gave hands and feet to the dreams of its visionary pastor, Sam Williams, and the rest of the creative staff team. How does your team function together?

Have you learned to rely on one another's strengths? Or are you attempting a team-sized task by yourself? What strengths and abilities is your team missing, and what must you discover or re-align to fill the void?

Partnerships

Although many churches are independent and nondenominational, since New Testament days most communities of faith have related primarily to other like-minded or like-mission fellowships. Here we address denominational partnerships and mission type partnerships between new churches and more established ones. These relationships can be really beneficial. For example, new churches receive support from many partnering sources. However, sometimes the relationships are difficult, as the partnering church or agency feels a need to impose extrabiblical parameters. Partnering organizations are responsible to many people whose reputation they honor and whose resources they steward, which means they are usually required to exert some kind of control and insist on some kind of accountability.

How does this affect you? First, do not anticipate a perfect alignment between you and all of your partners, especially those with whom you do not have a close personal relationship. However, even the imperfectly aligned relationship should always seek healthy relationships in the midst of this reality, like being flexible on issues that are negotiable. Second, the more new ground you break, the more important it can be that you forge trust relationships with your partners. It will be tempting to lie low and not offer others the opportunity to view your design experiments, and in some cases that's wise. But if others know your heart they are more likely to be supportive, even in cases where they don't understand your vision, values, or methods. Finally, walk in integrity. Initiate and gratefully accept healthy partnerships without compromising what God has asked you to do.

Financial Realities

We have mentioned Del Cerro Baptist Church in San Diego. Besides tripling in ten years, this church successfully started at least one church a year during the same period of time (1985–1995). Del Cerro was property-bound, with three Sunday morning services meeting in a small worship facility. There was no room for a new building, and no money to build elsewhere, but the congregation believed God wanted them to continue sharing Christ in their community. As a result, Del Cerro re-aligned around the worship facility problem by sending people out to start new churches. This will always be Del Cerro's legacy.

What are the financial realities around which you will design, refine, or re-align? One of the churches in Allan's network considers its budget as sacred. Its people will not and cannot make financial decisions without a budget. Some churches handle money more fluidly, and for others the idea of a budget is completely foreign. How do finances affect your church? Some models rely on really deep pockets and deep sacrifices in order to function, while others require just a little. Does this matter to you? How is God providing for you and your family?

Will the context in which God placed you ever sustain a fully paid staff? Does timing correlate with money in your situation? For example, if you are starting a new church in a culture with which you are not familiar, have you factored in the months it can take before the church starts producing income? Page Street Church in San Francisco is composed of mostly homeless or semihomeless adults. Even if outside support were available, what dynamics of change would emerge if a pastor there were fully funded? In the network of eighteen churches and almost one thousand active followers of Christ that Allan is a part of, only two pastors have a full salary, and they raise much of their own support. Many churches that are organized around mission choose not to support staff salaries because doing so inhibits their capacity to reproduce quickly. Carefully consider what you believe about the use of money in your context, and ask God how to make wise decisions that are right for your church and consistent with your biblical and strategic values.

Cultural Considerations

We have already introduced you to Jim, the artist who is in the process of re-aligning how he leads his church so that he can be truer to how God created him. But here's the catch; it would do no good for Jim to reconfigure the church around his own passions if they did not also match the culture where he ministers. The United States and Canada today, as well as much of the rest of the world, are experiencing stunning cultural shifts. Almost every church is navigating cultural shifts around lifestyle, language, generational differences, worldviews, and religion. What does this look like in your situation? Around what kinds of cultural realities will you design, refine, or re-align? Here is an example of how one kind of church might deal with issues related to cultural shift.

It is easier to plant or grow churches in monocultures than in multicultural environments. Perhaps, if you live and work in a multicultural urban area, you have already discovered this. Right now, maybe alignment for you means helping your church move out of the city into a less complex, quickly growing suburb where you can construct a larger building with a big parking lot and attract a larger constituency. But wait: Are there any other possibilities? Maybe God is leading your church to move, but you have narrowed your options too quickly. What can a city church do that a suburban church can't? Who can an urban church touch that a suburban church can't? How can the members of an urban church stretch in ways suburban church members cannot? Have you considered the potential of multiple language congregations in one building, the possibility of the wealthy and the poor working and worshipping together, a weekday service for people who work in the city but live in the suburbs, an outreach to the city through the arts or an Internet café, turning your facility into a multiuse, twenty-four/seven community ministry center, using the church as a base but not always the place from which worship and ministry radiate? Are there other options, or is God calling you to abandon the city?

Culture is not a problem; it's an opportunity. It is the gophers that attract rare red-tailed hawks, the bees that pollinate the flowers, and the plants we call weeds because they grow in places we did not dictate. Of all the things we could say about culture-based reality checks, perhaps the most needed alignment is that the human heart must be in alignment with the will of God. Every other alignment follows.

11

ORGANIZING BY DESIGN

*I now believe that CEOs and managers must know
Design Thinking to do their jobs. CEOs must be
designers and use their methodologies to actually
run companies.... Design Thinking is the new
Management Methodology. I think managers have
to* become *designers, not just hire them. I think
CEOs have to embrace design thinking, not just hire
someone who gets it.*
—BRUCE NUSSBAUM, ASSISTANT MANAGING EDITOR,
BUSINESSWEEK[1]

IN THE BEGINNING, God created the heavens and the earth and
then began giving order to a world that was formless and empty. He
intentionally organized relationships between people and Himself,
human and nonhuman life, husbands and wives, and children and
parents. He organized time into patterns of day and night, work
and rest, and life, death, and eternity. He organized every atom,
cell, and cellular network, every planet, star, galaxy, and physical
force in ways that cannot help but reflect who He is. He looked at
the universe He had designed and called it good. Our friends who
are not Christian, Jewish, or Muslim may be surprised to find out
that all three faiths believe God is both the Designer and the design
intent of the universe. By design intent, we mean that all things are
from Him, by Him, and for Him (Rom. 11:36). God is the meaningful content around which everything else is structured.

Because we are made in the image of God, people are born organizers. Human beings have been organizing since almost the beginning of our existence. We all organize aspects of our lives— planning for the future, handling finances, arranging a wedding. The design process is a more sophisticated form of organizing. It encompasses defining needs, articulating ways to address those needs, deciding which elements to include or reject, organizing how those elements relate to each other, and prioritizing them to reflect some greater purpose and set of values.

The purpose of this chapter is to introduce new lenses through which church leaders can examine the organizations they serve. Many of you work within the context of some existing ecclesial paradigm, institution, or system. Some of you are passionate about your work and want to keep learning new skills that will help you minister effectively through the life stages of the church you love. Others of you are less enamored of your church or denomination as an organization, but you sense that God has placed you where you are for a reason. Perhaps you are frustrated with hierarchies or endless committee meetings, but you are content to follow the Apostle Paul's advice: "Let each person lead the life that the Lord has assigned to him, and to which God has called him" or her (1 Cor. 7:17). However, sometimes you are caught in an organizational system where it seems impossible to solve problems and move toward the vision to which God has called you.

We want to help all of you by offering tools that can forge practical, hopeful paths toward your goals and dreams.

Defining Our Scope

Although there are a variety of topics related to design that are essential to the identity of good organizations (such as the nature and meaning of leadership, or the formation of vision, purpose, and strategies), they are outside the scope of this book. The specific void we seek to address in this chapter is the organization's design. We want to help refiners and re-aligners continue to work through existing options in new ways. Churches are generally unfamiliar with the idea of organizational design, so we think that exposure to these concepts will help strengthen and improve your church's organizational structure. We also want to give innovators (designers) the same set of tools. This process will better prepare them for next steps, to be addressed in the last chapter of this book.

The act of designing, let us repeat, has to do with deciding which elements are included or rejected, organizing how those elements relate to each other, and choosing how they are prioritized to intentionally reflect some greater purpose and set of values. Apple's Steve Jobs says, "In most people's vocabularies, design means veneers."[2] We will not be talking much about veneers, or cosmetic embellishments such as candles, incense, music style, and logo. These are usually only skin-deep indicators of what organizational design expert Tom Peters calls "soul."[3] So how would you explain the soul of your church? Is it about helping people find a way of life in Christ? multiplying disciples? aligning with what you understand as the purposes and priorities of God? Identifying the soul of your church helps begin to engage the design process because it reminds you about what you really want and hope will happen.

Understanding the Process

In previous chapters, we discussed individuals (self), communities, cultures, and theology. We asked you to make decisions about how they play out in your particular context. Next we presented a palette of models and considered how they aligned with personal and theological values. We gauged them against practical reality checks with the goal of discovering alignment between these elements. Now we would like to introduce you to a design process that can help you organize around these elements. To do this, we invented "Joe," a man with a dream.

Joe's Story

Joe is employed as a programmer, and his fiancée, Maria, is an office manager at the same business. After work, they frequent some local restaurants and spend time planning their wedding as they eat. They are familiar with each other's favorite restaurants and understand one another's taste in food. It takes no more than a text message to know when and where they will meet. The only question they are asking is, "Where will we eat tonight so that we can spend time planning our wedding?" The values reflected in Joe and Maria's meal planning process are maximum flexibility, minimum problem solving, high reproducibility, plus their food preferences. Decision making is really simple.

But Joe has other aspirations besides planning for a wedding. He has a goal of developing a caring community with the people who live in his large, apartment complex macrocommunity. He wonders how to make that happen, and he determines that eating a meal with some of his neighbors would help achieve his goal. So he invites his nearest neighbors over for dinner. He now needs to decide what that dinner might look like. His decision-making process embraces five domains of information:

1. *Self:* Joe is a creative person and a good cook. He does not like to bake.
2. *Microcommunity:* Maria does not cook but likes Joe's idea.
3. *Culture:* The couple Joe wants to befriend are from India. Joe guesses that they do not eat beef and may not eat meat at all. Joe was raised on Memphis soul food.
4. *Theology:* Joe is committed to the principles of hospitality, missional living, and practices of creation care that lead him to eat local, organic food.
5. *Reality checks:* Joe needs to budget both time and money. Taking the couple out to eat is not an option. Spending a lot of time cooking a meal is not an option either. Maria will not be helping him cook.

What does Joe decide to do about dinner? He would have liked to cook Indian food out of respect for his neighbors' palates, but he's not confident in his ability to reproduce an authentic-tasting Indian meal. So he decides to invite them for a humble fare of home-cooked, Southern food that reflects his own heritage. Because he has cooked meals like this dozens of times, he can prepare it quickly. He phones to ask if the neighbors are vegetarian and discovers that they eat fish. Joe decides on a wintry Georgia menu: fried fish, black-eyed peas, mustard greens, and sweet potatoes. Because he doesn't bake, Joe decides on ice cream for dessert and asks Maria to stop by a neighborhood creamery on the way to his house to pick up several of their locally made flavors. He purchases food the day before the event from a local organic market. No problem. This event is still simply structured and highly reproducible. Joe could continue meeting each neighbor family in the same way, and eventually he would know everyone.

We all process information just like Joe. We consider various domains of choice, starting with the elements that are either the most important to us or the least flexible. In Joe's case, the three inflexible elements are time, money, and his guests' dietary needs. Along with those, he considers three other critical factors: his comfort level in food preparation, his philosophy of food, and the sort of help he thinks he can get from Maria. Joe's decision grew out of the alignment of all of those elements.

Now let's suppose that Joe decides to invite his whole building of six families for a New Year's Day gathering. What changes, and how do those changes affect his decision-making process? We offer a new piece of information about microcommunity: Maria's mother is of Mexican heritage, and she loves nothing better than making tamales and beans for a New Year's crowd. Nothing else has changed, except time has passed and now Joe and Maria are married.

Joe asks Maria's mother to prepare some tamales and vegetarian-style beans for the Indian neighbors. His values regarding local, organic food are not challenged; he simply purchases the food Maria's mother needs to cook the meal. Joe just needs to prepare a salad, buy dessert, and remember to invite Maria's mother to the celebration. He approaches this situation with simple but centralized coordination. By inviting six families, Joe is able to meet people more quickly, and he is also able to connect them with one another.

In our next scenario, it's Easter. The residents of Joe and Maria's building want to do something together to celebrate, and they decide on an outdoor picnic with an egg hunt for the children. Neighbors in every building in the complex are interested and want to join the fun. How do the specific details of this event change how Joe approaches it? Nothing has changed in the domains of personhood or microcommunity, but there are other new elements to consider.

Culture: The residents of the complex are culturally diverse, representing many ages, lifestyles, and ethnicities. These largely middle-class families and singles live in six buildings, each containing six apartments.

Theology: Nobody except Joe really cares if the food is local and organic. They are not particularly committed to hospitality, but they are intrigued with the idea of becoming more of a real neighborhood.

Reality checks: Joe is still busy and still has very little money, but now the task is potentially more complex and more expensive.

What needs to happen?

Joe has now reached the limits of his own capacity to organize, so he relies on Maria's strength. She makes every building in the complex responsible for a part of the meal: drinks, salads, appetizers, main dishes, hot vegetables, and desserts. She posts a sign-up list for setup, cleanup, and activities. This idea works fine, but Joe has to compromise some of his personal values. The event takes more time to plan, it is less reproducible and more complicated, and it requires more organizing skills. In addition, because so many people with differing sets of values are pitching in with food, decoration, and cleanup, Joe is no longer able to maintain his value of creation care and eating local, organic food. He is able to meet many people, but he is so busy with the details of the event that there is little capacity for developing friendships. Because Joe's understanding of hospitality is related to opening his home, hospitality in a strict sense is not fostered in the context of this event. Yet despite these compromises, many more people are connected to one another than ever before in the apartment complex's history. He never meant to organize the neighbors, but it has happened. Joe asks himself whether the compromise was worth it.

What are Joe's best options in light of his original goal of helping to develop a caring community? What ways of moving forward best align with his goals, his new marriage, his values, and his gifts? Should he move to form some sort of formal neighborhood association with elected people coordinating activities? Should he retreat to simplify, perhaps connecting mostly with people who live in his own building?

What would you do? Would you adapt your original intent on the basis of the new situation, or revert back to it? Your next steps may be quite different from Joe's. Notice that from his problem Joe can decide whether he wants to innovate (design something new) or simply refine or re-align. Our solution is that he approaches his decision making from the inside out.

Designing from the Inside Out

Information architect Jesse James Garrett is the author of a now classic work about website development, *The Elements of User Experience*. In his book, he introduced a way to think about constructing websites in a way that satisfies both the strategic objectives of the site owner and the needs of the site's users. Garret introduces five planes, which build on one another, each influencing how decisions are made.

1. The *surface* plane: This includes images and text that are initially visible or may be clicked on by the end user who comes in contact with the site. (visual design)
2. The *skeleton* plane: Beneath the surface, the components of individual pages such as objects, buttons, text, and photos are arranged so that the design intent of the page is maximized for effect and efficiency. (information design)
3. The *structure* plane: The structure plane defines how different aspects of the site work together, including things like how the user browses or navigates within a site, and the organizing principle of the site. (interaction design and information architecture)
4. The *scope* plane: The scope plane answers the questions "What will be built? What will not be built?" It deals with specific requirements related to scope and functionality, and it serves strategic objectives. (functional specifications and content requirements)
5. The *strategy* plane: Decisions made on this plane are determined by two things: the specific objective(s) of the site owner and the contextualized, segmented needs of site users. (user needs and site objectives)[4]

Although these planes are listed here from the outside (concrete) to the inside (abstract), as the website user experiences them the competent website designer addresses them from the inside out: strategy plane first and surface plane last.

Using ideas taken from Garrett's model, we have drawn our own version of his inside-out design model (see Figure 11.1). His interest is specific to website development, but there are some clear parallels between Garrett's paradigm and church designing. The first design layer we addressed in this book was the human self. We began there because before our readers make any other decisions, we want them to have already wrestled with issues of identity and personal values. We moved into the community chapter next because in many ways the people who come together around mission (the microcommunity communitas) are an extension of self. The identity of your team matters deeply, because these are the people pouring out their lives for the sake of the Kingdom, and God is always the starting place and central focus for designing churches. Here is how we choose to engage the design process, starting inside out, from abstract to concrete, and from grand scale to the smallest detail.

FIGURE 11.1. AN INSIDE-OUT DESIGN PROCESS.

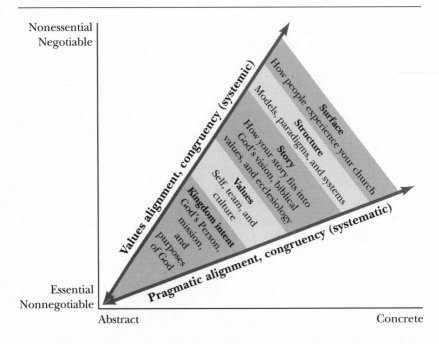

Kingdom Intent Plane

We begin with the design environment: God is doing something. He has a cosmic plan, and the big picture belongs to Him. The Kingdom intent plane relates to the content of Chapter Four. It reflects the church designer's commitment that everything else in the design is subject to God's person, activity, purposes, and mission. Biblical values and a biblically based ecclesiology are sorted out on this plane and must reverberate throughout the entire design.

Values Plane

The values plane addresses the elements of self (who you are), community (who you are doing this with—meaning, the team starting or leading the church with you), and culture (who you are doing this in light of), filtered through a set of reality checks. What values are related to each element, and how do they fit together? What values are prioritized? Are any values articulated here also values on the Kingdom plane?

Story plane

The story plane indicates how the design team's story (their hopes and dreams) fits into God's story. Your story should be visionary and hopeful, transcending model, culture, and even values. This plane is where you consider and clarify your operating principle, the question "What kind of church will you start (or do you currently lead)?" It is also the plane where specific biblical values and theological calling (serving the poor, promoting justice, human wholeness and healing) are affirmed. What are you hoping for? Are your beliefs and priorities clearly addressed, or are they merely assumed in the story?

Structure Plane

Here, on the structure plane, decisions are finally made about how a specific church will organize in a way that is true to its beliefs, a fit for the team, culturally responsive and engaged, plus realistic yet faith-filled. This is the plane where models (forms or examples you have in mind), paradigms (your set of assumptions or concepts regarding church), and systems (how you see the components working together) are agreed, old models are adopted or refined, and new ones spring to life. The decisions you make here will either help or hinder the capacity of structure to serve the mission, vision, and values of the church. Much of the rest of this chapter will begin to answer the question, "Which structures best fit with our God-given dream?"

Surface Plane

The surface plane is the "skin" that determines what Garrett calls the user experience in website design. It includes anything from forms of worship to the church name. Literally it can mean any way that people who come into contact with your church experience it. Surface plane decisions should always flow out of information gleaned from the other planes, but the consistency we hope for is rare. Examples of inconsistency include a church that says it wants to be multiethnic but whose leadership is from a single ethnic group, or the church that claims to value beauty but meets in an aesthetically uninteresting space. What would people surmise about your beliefs and values just by experiencing your church on the surface?

Creating Better Organizations

In the beginning of this chapter, we said that one of our chapter goals was to offer new lenses for thinking about existing options in new ways. The section about organizing principles in the previous chapter is one option. It is based on asking fresh questions and organizing around what matters. Now we offer three more tools. First, we introduce you to the concept of organizational metaphors. Metaphors are simply pictures that help people conceptualize things in new ways. Then we present two ways to think about structure. Many churches and denominational structures need to reconfigure their structures because they have become very different organizations from what they were when they began.

Organizational Metaphors

The Bible uses a number of metaphors for thinking about what it means to be the people of God: household, flock, body, bride, and royal priesthood are among the most familiar. Each metaphor suggests a slightly different angle of our relationship to God; taken together, they provide a more complete understanding of what that relationship should look like. For example, a flock, though tenderly cared for by the shepherd, may just seem smelly and dumb, but the added dimension of priesthood transforms the image by elevating and dignifying it. Lakoff and Johnson offer: "We define our reality in terms of metaphors and then proceed to act on the basis of the metaphors. We draw inferences, set goals, make commitments, and execute plans, all on the basis of how we in part structure our experience, consciously and unconsciously, by means of metaphor."[5]

Gareth Morgan, author of the book *Images of Organization*,[6] discussed eight complex metaphors he has observed in organizations. He says that each helps by offering a perspective that may be useful for various situations or life cycle phases. No one metaphor is meant to be complete or sufficient in and of itself; each has its strengths and weaknesses. Here are the metaphors on Morgan's list that we see most frequently embraced by churches:

1. *Organizations as machines.* The worldview that enabled bureaucracies, scientific management systems, and routinization spawned churches after its own kind. Under this metaphor, the best churches are those that are goal-oriented, perform well, and are reliable, efficient, predictable, and productive. Increased production capacity is directly linked to a greater need to distribute (sell or give away) whatever is produced and a corresponding need to find buyers.

2. *Organizations as organisms.* Unlike machines, organisms are alive and seek to continue to survive. In that organisms are also committed to both growth and reproduction, they have something in common with the machine metaphor's commitment to productivity. It is noteworthy that the words *organism* and *organization* have the same root, *organon,* which is the Greek word for instrument. For centuries, people have considered nonhuman organisms to be their instruments.

3. *Organizations as brains.* Organizations may also be viewed as information processing and learning environments that broker information. Processes are based on cognition—knowing and assenting to the right information. Hence the information-centered way most churches help people to become

better followers of Jesus. Preaching, teaching, discipleship programs, and seminary training are evidence that churches are comfortable with the brain metaphor of organizations.

4. *Organizations as cultures.* By this we mean entire systems of rules, laws, norms, traditions, beliefs, art, morals, and more. Organizations create internal cultures, and even churches have their own cultures by which they can judge whether others are insiders or outsiders. How would you describe the culture of your church? How does it fit within your larger denominational culture?[7]

Structure Tools

Linda works with four other strategists who live elsewhere in the Bay Area. They are organized *divisionally* according to the ethno-linguistic groups with whom they work. This framework was put in place by the California Southern Baptist Convention many years ago, when California was less diverse, the Bay Area was less populated, its city centers were less connected to each other, and multiculturalism was less valued in California. Because the Bay Area is a very different place from what it was three decades ago, the strategists began realizing they were weighed down by their structure.

As they searched for a new way of organizing, several possibilities surfaced. They could have organized *geographically*, with each person responsible for a region. This would not have worked, however, because it would not have taken advantage of their skills in relating to particular people groups. Another option would have been to organize *functionally* around particular tasks. Each could have been responsible for the whole Bay Area in some area of the ministry (recruitment, deployment, basic training, partnership building, mentoring). This organizational structure, however, was incompatible with the strategists' job descriptions because they each already had a functional job description based on a particular people group. Another option would be to create a *matrix* structure, with each person keeping his or her current divisional role but also engaging a geographical or functional matrix that cut across the whole. In other words, they could each perform the tasks of their assigned job description while also assuming a geographical or a task-oriented role.

The strategists began organizing around a matrix structure, but in light of the complexity of the Bay Area and the comprehensive nature of their task they found it still had only limited possibilities. Now, they are in the process of organizing around a *team* structure. They will work around vision, values, and mission according to divisional tasks, spiritual gifts, and special team projects. For example, Howard Burkhart, who is a great administrator, organized the details of a large student summer mission trip. It benefited church planters who relate organizationally to all five strategists, not just Howard.

The Bay Area Planting Team is also in the process of selecting a support team of paid, commissioned, and volunteer personnel. Every structure they create together will serve and carry the vision, values, and mission. This transition could have happened years ago, had the team been familiar with the variety of organizational structures available to them. A design question for you: Are you stuck in part because your organizational structure is insufficient for the vision of the church? What might be released if another structure were employed? If you are newly organizing, is it possible to organize provisionally for the current stage of work, and shift occasionally with new stages of development?

Aspects of Church Life

Another way of thinking about church structure is to consider some visible, predictable aspects of church life (Figure 11.2):

1. Sacramental and celebrative (worship, vows, intercession, confession)
2. Relationship-oriented (encouragement, community, fellowship, covenant)
3. Transformational (evangelism, church starting, mission and missions, activism)
4. Structural (finances, administration, membership, programs, policies)

The figures on these pages depict how it is possible to draw the organizing structures of various kinds of churches according to the degree to which they live in these four quadrants (see Figures 11.3, 11.4, and 11.5). For example, a house church may mostly concern itself in the relationship quadrant, but its decision to be missional means that a good deal of its new identity moves to the transformational quadrant (Figure 11.3). A highly

FIGURE 11.2. ASPECTS OF CHURCH LIFE (DESCRIPTIVE, NOT PRESCRIPTIVE).

Transformational	Structural/Organizational
Evangelism	Conducting regular meetings
Discipleship	Wineskins
Mission	Programs and practices
Justice, mercy ministries	Legal matters
Personal spiritual growth	Decision making
Prayer	Finances, administration
Earth stewardship	Policies and procedures
Exemplification of transformation	Roles, hierarchy, position
Agent of the kingdom of God	Denominational relationships
Social concerns	Membership
Healing	Keeper of tradition
Leadership roles: transformational (apostle, evangelist, teacher)	*Leadership roles: positional (bishop, overseer)*
Some images of the church: salt and light, ministers of reconciliation	Some images of the church: body, temple, steward
Sacramental/Celebrative	**Relational**
Worship	Interdependence
Celebrations	Interpersonal relationships
Sacraments	Mutuality, encouragement
Intercession	Community
Christian practices	*Ecclesia, koinonia, oikos*
Piety, holiness	Covenant
Mystery	Caregiving
Ritual	Gathering
Confession	Reconciliation
Leadership roles: seeing, hearing, accessing God, eschatological perspective (priest, prophet)	Peacekeeping
Some images of the church: mystery, royal priesthood, holy nation, church of God, community of the spirit	*Leadership roles: servant, counselor (deacon, pastor, shepherd)*
	Some images of the church: community, fellowship of the saints, family of God, brothers and sisters

liturgical mainline church may live more in the sacramental and celebrative, as well as in some aspects of the transformational quadrant (Figure 11.4). A seeker church may live mostly in the transformational quadrant, with the relational and sacramental-celebrative areas serving and submitting to the transformational quadrant. Ideally, structure would serve the other three quadrants, stretched around them like a flexible, permeable membrane (Figure 11.5).

Within every church, God places people who lead out of a set of gifts that match the quadrant with which that particular church most identifies. Evangelists and apostles serve the transformational quadrant, where the church acts out its identity as the sent people of God. Priests, worship leaders, and prophets serve the church in the sacramental-celebrative quadrant, leading a church into its identity as a worshipping holy priesthood. Shepherds and deacons move the church toward fellowship and community formation.

FIGURE 11.3. MISSIONAL HOUSE CHURCH ORGANIZING STRUCTURE.

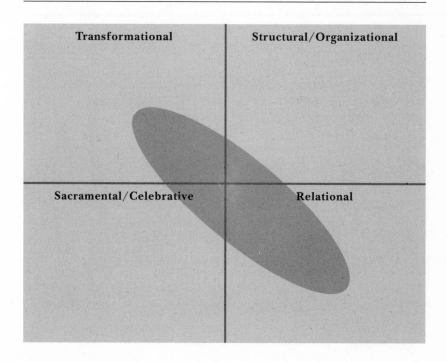

Transformational

Structural/Organizational

Sacramental/Celebrative

Relational

FIGURE 11.4. MAINLINE/LITURGICAL CHURCH ORGANIZING STRUCTURE.

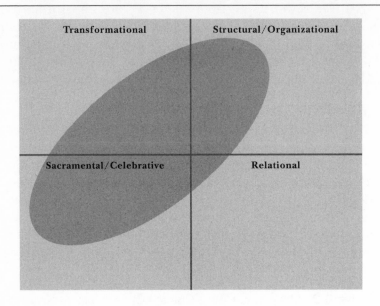

FIGURE 11.5. SEEKER CHURCH ORGANIZING STRUCTURE.

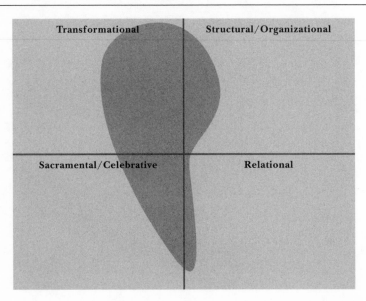

In which quadrants does your church live most fully? What does this say about your church's values, calling, mission, or operating principle? Does this line up with your biblical understanding of church?

Design Wisdom for Organizations

Structures Need to Be Responsive

In 2008, IBM conducted a global study of one thousand CEOs and public sector leaders that showed eight out of ten CEOs claiming "their organizations were facing substantial or very substantial change over the next three years."[8] Churches exist in this same change environment of the times. More important, churches need to be ready to change in relationship to God's direction and factors such as their needs, goals, objectives, context, and leadership. Wal-Mart (regardless of whatever else you might think about the business) convenes its management staff *every single week* to take a hard look at themselves, examine trends, and formulate immediate responses that affect their operations.

Most churches examine themselves only occasionally and rarely change in reality. Only a few of our traditions are biblically based, but even without a biblical basis many cling to them as if they were equivalent to Christ's commands. A small church's budget declines because local job loss affects members, but it never amends its yearly budget so that it can function within the present financial reality. A church grows rapidly but neglects starting new groups to assimilate new members. A community transitions ethnically, but the ethnic composition of its local church never does. In each situation, church structure is so inflexible that the church is unresponsive to new factors that indicate a need for change.

The Whole Is More Than the Sum of Its Parts

A building is more than a collection of bricks and mortar; buildings made with bricks require some kind of congruent ordering in relationship to laws of physics, building codes, and design plans. Buildings are also more than the correct ordering, designing, aligning, and joining of parts. They are places to live, monuments

176 CHURCH TURNED INSIDE OUT

to history, and memories of family. We, the church, are "built on the foundation of the apostles and prophets, Christ Jesus himself being the cornerstone, in whom the whole structure, being joined together, grows into a holy temple in the Lord" (Eph. 2:20–21). Each of us is a living stone (1 Peter 2:5). We matter to the whole and belong to the whole of what God is doing. In what ways does the organizing mechanism of your church reflect that each member is valuable to the whole? In what way does it reflect the opposite? How will you and your church organize to participate in the Kingdom?

It's About Wine, *and* It's About Wineskins

"Neither do men pour new wine into old wineskins. If they do, the skins will burst, the wine will run out and the wineskins will be ruined. No, they pour new wine into new wineskins, and both are preserved" (Matt. 9:17).

What on earth was Jesus talking about? He seemed to be interested in preserving both wine *and* skins. The relationship between the two, however, is that the wineskin exists for the wine, and not the other way around. The new wine, most people agree, is the substantive, always-fresh gospel of the Kingdom. Everything else is secondary, including traditions, buildings, constitutions, membership. All of these are wineskins. We must remain mindful of what is most important, remembering that the best use of structure is to help facilitate the body of Christ and its mission to become all it can be. What does structure serve? It serves the gospel. Can you tell the difference between the wine and the wineskins in the church organization of which you are a part? Which is servant, and which is master? The point for church designers, refiners, and re-aligners is not to discard all wineskins, but to reexamine them in light of their ability to support the nature and mission of the church. Saying that, however, I will add that the next chapter of this book again addresses the topic of wineskins. These issues point naturally to the very heart of innovative design. In 1975, Howard Snyder called this design question "the problem of wineskins."[9]

12

A NEW WAY OF ORGANIZING

I had been taught to work like others and after careful thinking I decided that I wasn't going to spend my life doing what had already been done.
—GEORGIA O'KEEFE[1]

SEVENTY YEARS BEFORE the "green movement" in North America became politically correct, biologist Rachel Carson dedicated her life to environmental causes. Her 1962 classic, *Silent Spring,* generated an outburst of controversy concerning the widespread agricultural use of chemical pesticides. The industry responded with a sharp counterattack that pesticides were responsible for the elimination of diseases such as yellow fever, malaria, and typhus around the world; without pesticides, agricultural production would suffer unfathomably, and many would die from malnutrition or starvation. The controversy catapulted, and thousands of people began to see their planet with new eyes.

Despite the dominant mechanistic worldview of her day, Carson's background as a botanist/ecologist helped her operate out of a more organic paradigm. Paradigm shifting happens when people have new information that makes them see the world differently, or when they begin to ask fresh questions that are based on the needs and opportunities presented by new realities. Carson helped people begin the process of paradigm shifting, and because of her writing people across the world began to reimagine how people could live differently on earth. She wrote: "For most of us, knowledge of our world comes largely through sight, yet we look about with such unseeing eyes that we are partially blind. One way to open your eyes is to ask yourself, 'What if I had never seen this before?'"[2]

This chapter is about new ways of seeing and asking questions, leading to new ways of being and organizing as God's people. Ultimately this is a designer's chapter. The primary role of design thinking is not to take things that already exist and reshuffle them in more beneficial, beautiful, enriching, or productive ways, although that is a valid aspect of design. At the very heart of design thinking is a process that helps reframe questions, encounter problems innovatively, generate new possibilities, and experiment with options. For God's people, the end goal of this process is transformation in keeping with God's priorities.

A New Way of Seeing

Transformation, it turns out, is a new way of thinking being addressed at the periphery of design. On the last day of 2008, Bruce Nussbaum, one of America's foremost design experts, wrote an article for *BusinessWeek* titled "'Innovation' Is Dead. Herald the Birth of 'Transformation' as the Key Concept for 2009." This epitaph was a startling proclamation in light of several previous decades of design wisdom that claimed that design *is* innovation. He wrote that "'innovation' died in 2008" because everyone started "conflating it with change, technology, design, globalization, trendiness, and anything 'new.'" Nussbaum expressed doubt that innovation alone has the capacity to navigate the future because "it is too narrow to generate radical alternative options and build risk-taking frontier skills needed to remake and restructure our lives, our economies and our countries. . . . We need a deeper, more robust concept. 'Transformation' captures the key changes already under way and can help guide us into the future."[3]

Nussbaum ends with an appeal and a question: "'Transformation' takes the best of 'design thinking' and 'innovation' and integrates them into a strategic guide for the unknowable and uncertain years ahead. . . . As a concept, it needs more detail and texture. What do you think we should add to it? Does it work for you?"[4]

Nussbaum wrote this article in the midst of widespread, systemic economic and social turmoil. He advocated a "radical transformation of our systems" framed in a context within which "change now!" is the inevitable outcry that seems to embrace almost every arena of life.[5] Is the church up to the challenge? Are you ready for change?

During the last part of the nineteenth century and most of the twentieth, the majority of social and organizational theorists believed that the mechanistic modern organization was the best solution for achieving social order.

> The organizationalists looked upon society as an order of functions, a utilitarian construct of integrated activity, a means for focusing human energy in combined effort. . . . The symbol of organization was power . . . organization signifies a method of social control, a means for imparting order, structure and regularity.[6]

As modernism began crumbling, however, an emerging reactionary stream also began doubting some aspects of modern organizations. Organizational studies expert Michael Reed suggests, "Both the technical effectiveness and moral virtue of 'formal' or 'complex' organizations are called into question by institutional and intellectual transformations that push inexorably towards social fragmentation, political disintegration, and ethical relativism."[7]

Reed goes on to call this a "historic juncture" for organizational theory when " all the old ideological 'certainties' and technical 'fixes' that once underpinned their 'discipline' are fundamentally being called into question."[8] Reed is far from alone in this opinion. Simply put, the classical ways of organizing are no longer ironclad rules for organizations, including church organizations that borrowed those structures and their underlying worldview.

The new worldview, which came into being as a reaction to the abuses of the mechanistic universe, is more compatible with the idea of a living universe. The word *organic*, for example, has now become standardized, commercialized, and baptized into the common vernacular. This term, which means "living, vital, elemental, essential, and fundamental," seems new, but it is actually not a new idea for organizations. One hundred years ago, the eminent French sociologist Emile Durkheim wrote about the role religion played in society's transition from mechanical to "organic solidarity." As a legal theorist, Oliver Wendell Holmes proposed an organic approach to law from a judicial perspective. In 1908, Woodrow Wilson said, "We have been living under an impossible thing—a Newtonian system of government. A government is not a mechanism, but a living thing."[9]

For most people, the term *organic* generates positive meanings such as healthy, natural, real, wholesome, and alive. In scientific terms, organic compounds are produced by living things, and like all living things they contain carbon. Churches that have named themselves "organic" embrace this nomenclature because what they want is a natural, simple, missional process that is identified with a Jesus way of life in community.

Inorganic compounds, on the other hand, are generally produced by nonliving natural processes and do not contain carbon. We have never heard anyone call churches "inorganic" because, of course, everyone knows deep inside that churches are people and not buildings, and life is what all churches are about.

Instead of the term *inorganic,* it is common to call churches that own buildings, pay pastors, operate budgets, and conduct programs "institutional" churches. Churches with these features have not chosen this nomenclature for themselves. Why would they? *Institution* calls forth many negative connotations: establishment, hierarchy, buildings, conformity, uniformity, and lack of personal attention. Are there really only two ways to be a church? Outside of some ultraconservative Christian cultures, nobody really believes that there is some notion of church differentiated by things such as buildings and budgets. At the same time, it is problematic that others question the authentic faith of the millions of people who don't practice Christianity in an institutional church context. What are the new questions we must ask that will help us find our way through this stalemate?

A New Metaphor for Organizing

Organizational experts Margaret Wheatley and Myron Kellner-Rogers based their book *A Simpler Way* on the question, "How could we organize human endeavor if we developed a different understanding of how life organizes itself?"[10] Their question echoes the design question we two are asking about the Church. We both love the ideas behind the concept of organic, but the term is not in itself a comprehensive enough metaphor to capture the idea we want to propose. At the leading edge of culture, there is an exciting dialogue about a way of organizing that is more compatible with how God ordered the natural world. This concept, referred to as living systems, is more about a way of being together than it is about completing certain tasks, even the worthy task of mission. The ideas it embraces are present in disciplines as diverse as science, art, philosophy, politics, architecture, nursing, and urban planning.

In the last several decades, the concept of living systems has been translated into the social sciences, including organizational design theory. It is another of the eight primary metaphors listed by Gareth Morgan, whose book *Images of Organization* we discussed in Chapter Eleven. What Morgan calls "flux and transformation" is a metaphor for rethinking organizations in light of new scientific insights such as chaos, complexity, and change. Living organizations are unique because individuals are unique; communities are not static, cultures are fluid, systems of belief are not identical, and God chooses to work in an infinite number of creative and life-giving ways.

To be clear, there is a huge distinction between an ecological, living-systems worldview and the use of a living-systems organizing metaphor. A Christian worldview is by definition Christ-centric. Metaphors are just tools for seeing. We remind you again that there are many metaphors for church in the New Testament (living stones, body, building, household, flock, army, and more). Each metaphor offers a perspective, and each stresses the vital relationships of individuals to the whole. A living system metaphor helps point toward what we already know is true about God's desire for His Church. Whatever name it goes by, it is the idea missiologist David Bosch was getting at when he proposed interdependence as a new paradigm for the emerging world:

> The individual is not a monad, but part of an organism. We live in one world in which the rescue of others is not possible. Only together is there salvation and survival. This includes not only a new relationship to nature, but also among humans. The "psychology of separateness" has to make way for an "epistemology of

participation." The "me generation" has to be superseded by the "us generation" [. . .] Here lies the pertinence of the rediscovery of the Church as Body of Christ and of the Christian mission as building a community of those who share a common destiny.[11]

Qualities Associated with Living Systems

Living systems carry the essential properties of life, so there are certain lifelike qualities we should anticipate being able to discover in any system we call "living." By *system* we mean that there is some sense of a coordinated whole or collective. Every living system contains recognizable interconnected properties that can also be described in relationship to the church: (1) wholeness, (2) networks, (3) processes (energy flow), (4) diversity, (5) resiliency, and (6) sustainability.

Wholeness

Systems thinking always involves a shift from the part to the whole. We have all heard the expression that the whole is greater than the sum of its parts, but what does it mean? It means that we miss the point by valuing A and valuing B, unless we pay attention to the conjunction "*and*" which bonds the two. In living systems, growth happens out of wholeness. God did not choose to grow people, for example, by starting with a skull and adding a brain, eyes, and other body parts. Everything needed for human growth was there from the beginning. The renowned Berkeley architect Christopher Alexander claimed "it is impossible to form anything that has the character of nature by adding preformed parts."[12] Because *organic* can apply to individual elements, a living systems metaphor implies the whole. This is the imagery of the body of Christ: the whole that functions in concert, the Shepherd who teaches the flock to mourn when even one lamb is lost. Frank Viola calls the church to wholeness: "The only basis for Christian fellowship is Christ plus nothing. The body of Christ minus nothing. The body of Christ alone."[13]

Networks

Individual organisms are made up of systems that are in themselves networks of networks. These networked systems engage, nourish, and nurture whole communities; they are inherently relational. Networks work well when there is a pattern of interdependency and collaboration between all real and potential entities within the system. Networks of networks are also decentralized. Instead of moving through hierarchies of layers to connect to each other, both networks and individual organisms connect with one another in myriad ways. This does not mean that nothing is centralized or hierarchical (for instance, humans have central nervous systems), but instead that whole systems of networks are decentralized and self-organized by choice.

In the San Francisco Bay Area, there are faith collectives composed of leaders from churches and church-helping organizations. There are networks of simple churches meeting and eating with megachurch hopefuls, fellowships of churches meeting across "party lines," church planters helping one another across denominations even when they are planting in the same part of town. There are also Christian businesspeople befriending new missionaries, and established pastors helping new ministers figure out how to live in their new city. The result is far from perfect, but the direction is right and is producing a healthy ecosystem for Kingdom life to flourish in the Bay Area.

Cyclical Processes

Design master Tom Peters illustrated "beautifully designed systems" in his book *Re-Imagine* by explaining the digestive systems of elephants. Because elephants process food inefficiently, their dung is rich with unprocessed foods. Peters described the natural habitat where termites burrow underground toward the elephants, and when they arrive deposit sand and carry away dung-food. It is a perfectly designed cycle of energy flow in that one species' waste is another's food and the other's waste disposal system.[14] Cycles of interdependency are found throughout living systems. In their book by the same name, living systems designers William McDonough and Michael Braungart call this a "cradle to cradle" process. Church networks can function like living systems, too. For example, leaders who are being raised up in Ethne's ecosphere need learning opportunities for ministry, including teaching and preaching. Churches in the network that need people to help them teach and preach then give the up-and-coming Ethne leaders the opportunity to learn. They choose partnership over isolation in dozens of ways. Like organisms, these churches cannot live alone.

Page Street Center Church in San Francisco also operates as a living system. The church is part of the larger whole of the center's activities, among them giving food and clothing to those in need and a drop-in center for mostly homeless youth. The church was birthed from the relationships that formed in these other activities, so the values embedded in the church's culture look like the values of the whole. The center is unique in that it embodies the concept that everybody has something to give and everybody has something to receive. Labor-intensive and client-driven, Page Street is a place where receivers become givers as clients invest back into the system.[15] When other churches visit, they are placed under the tutelage of client volunteers, and even served meals by them. Page Street has become well known among service providers in San Francisco for the healthy and sustainable flow of energy it generates.

Diversity

God created the world with incomprehensible diversity and left it for humans to enjoy, nurture, and protect. Sometimes however, we have treated the gift as if it were a nuisance: "Under the existing paradigm of manufacturing and development, diversity—an integral element of the natural world—is typically treated as a hostile force and a threat to design goals."[16]

In industry, the goal is to produce as much as possible (sometimes qualitatively better), as efficiently as possible, maximizing product and minimizing expense. Standardization is the result.

Although product diversity is created, it usually happens as a result of consumer expectations rather than from an appreciation of diversity. For example, builders design rows of houses to seem as if they are not cookie-cutter representations of one another, but they do so while at the same time disturbing the diversity of a natural habitat, replacing it with minimalist, efficient landscaping that helps sell homes.

Churches often operate out of the same efficiency paradigm, seeking to maximize productivity and efficiency, often at the expense of diversity. For example, when a denomination's bottom-line question for its agencies is "How many churches, how many new members, or how many baptisms did you produce?" the human response is to go after what is easy. This means that whatever is most difficult is ignored (complex urban areas, "unreached people groups," least responsive peoples) in favor of an easier short-term solution (homogeneity, new suburbs, rebaptizing people). This is not the message most of us want to convey, but the metaphors we live under create serious design flaws.

Resiliency

Resiliency, or the ability to weather the unexpected and recover from disturbances, is a concept associated with diversity. This is the same principle behind diversifying a financial portfolio. Diverse portfolios are better able to withstand the unpredictability of the market. Many sustainable agriculturists predict that "'resiliency' may someday replace 'efficiency' as the organizing principle of our economy. Our current economic system is designed to maximize outputs and minimize costs. (That's what we call efficiency.) Efficiency eliminates redundancy, which is abundant in nature, in favor of finding the one 'best' way of doing something—usually 'best' means most profitable over the short run—and then doing it that way and that way only." [17]

Resilient systems are adaptable and diverse. Instead of working to control external contexts in ways that ensure predictable results, resilient environments embrace the dynamics of change. One reason many people prefer to lead churches in suburbs rather than urban cores is that suburbs are more predictable.

Resilient systems, on the other hand, are diverse. They cannot thrive as monocultures. As an example, consider the cavendish, the common table banana, sometimes acclaimed as "the world's most perfect food." But now, after generations of genetic engineering, the cavendish, bred for efficiency, is too perfect and is therefore fast on its way to extinction. It turns out that the cavendish is not resilient. It is unable to withstand a widespread fungal bacteria that is killing it off as a species.

Sustainability

Sustainability is not so much a particular characteristic of living systems as it is a result of the design choices inherent in the system itself. Sustainability is about the right of every diverse species in the network to thrive according to its nature, while not taking that capacity away from other present and future organisms. Environments where these kinds of dynamic relationships exist are sustainable. Linda remembers a time when some new church planters joined an existing network that had grown out of ones that were more simply structured. The new planters wanted meetings to be more purposeful while the original network partners wanted to continue meeting informally around relationships. That night, Linda had a dream about a field that was full of low-lying grasses and native flowers. But a few elephants had wandered into the field, and by their sheer weight they were destroying the field. The meaning of the dream seemed clear. There needed to be some boundaries that allowed networking and interaction but also valued and took into consideration the varying nature of church planters. The group needed a new way of organizing that would better sustain what God was doing in the present tense, and what the team anticipated He would do in the future.

Lessons from an Ancient Forest

Founders Grove in California's Humboldt County State Park is home to some of the oldest, tallest trees anybody has ever seen. Some redwoods in this ancient forest soar so high that it is expected their branches host the kinds of life that have never been seen or studied by humans. The tallest of these trees is fallen, due to a storm that finally claimed its life at the close of the twentieth century. Close by, the world's second tallest tree still stands, offering layers and layers of leaf canopy to the cool, moist forest floor. Tourists take pictures at both places, no less amazed at the fallen giant than at the one still standing after more than two thousand years. There are dozens of trees almost as old, intermingled with newer growth, boasting an average age of more than three hundred years. Saplings are everywhere, feeding on the organic matter of decaying fallen trees that take as long as four hundred years to fully decay and return to the soil. Every tablespoon of dirt is teeming with life. The beauty of the forest is not only captured by the famed giant redwoods but also by the sustainable, Creator-designed biosystem that exists for the best interest of all forest life.

There are four defining features of trees in an ancient or all-age forest, wherever it is found. Dead, fallen trees supply rich organic matter that helps nourish the seeds that become the newest plants and trees. These fallen trees remind us of the ancients from which we derive our faith heritage, whether or not we acknowledge it. Old trees, dead or mostly dead but still standing, are another aspect of the forest. A multitude of birds and insects live in their branches, eat from their bark, and make their homes there. These are like some old churches, still standing but empty and void of the life they once knew, yet still able to offer the possibility of life to others. Their branches host meeting places for new-life congregations, offer ministry and service to their communities, furnish sacred space for prayer, and present stable, tangible evidence of the Kingdom of God. Their scars are our history, and the life they once lived helps us understand our past as well as reenvision our future.

Newer growth trees support life closer to the ground while they devote energy toward the process of someday becoming canopy-type trees; it is their DNA. Meanwhile, their branches are more reachable, are easier to glean from, and may be examined and critiqued more readily than those of older, taller trees. Like their botanical counterparts, new growth churches of the last several decades host life that has been visible, identifiable, quantifiable, and therefore easier for even newer churches to learn from. However, they are not the whole forest. Alone, they are more like an orchard or grove of same-age, same-type trees. Nobody calls a Christmas tree farm beautiful. Tree farms are designed for function, not beauty; they are intentionally monocultural and labor-intensive.

Every ancient forest also has multiple layers of canopy that supplies cool shade and offers protective shelter to other forms of life. It is the branches of these tall trees that host those life forms yet unknown even to people who study trees. But it is clear that not every botanical specimen in the forest is a canopy tree, or any kind of tree at all. The earth is spread with thousands upon thousands of rapidly growing ferns, draping vines, vivid mosses, and tiny flowering species, which represent to us the myriad life-giving small faith communities that we see flourishing across the country. All together, these living elements make up an ecosystem that offers promise and hope to future generations of both forest life and human life.[18]

The word *ecology* is coined from the Greek word for family or household (*oikos*). God's people represent an ecology in much the same way as a botanical ecosystem does. We are interdependent, and we need each other. We need to engage together in sustainable ways of life, respect one another's diversity, and stay mindful that we are connected to one another's past, present, and future. We need to imagine and take responsibility for stewarding our shared future, remembering that our own interwoven beauty pays tribute to God's handiwork and not our own. So how can we discover a shared ecosystem of faith that helps us know how to live in a way that maximizes promise and hope for all?

When we began writing this book, we were both skeptical about how to express with integrity our desire to be helpful to the larger body of Christ. There are expressions of church that are foreign to our own way of thinking, and others that more clearly represent us. How would we (or even could we) write so that designers, refiners, and re-aligners all felt affirmed and valued? We were not aiming for tolerance, because tolerance means there is no real challenge. It limits our interaction with one another and dissolves the poignancy of mutuality found in honest relationships. It's really not "all good." Christians need to be able to ask questions of one another and confront one another in the spirit of truth and love. The analogy of the Bride of Christ with which we began this inquiry was useful to us. We really do believe that there are many ways in which she can present herself as passionate and lovely before her Bridegroom. But the bride we know is not always beautiful. The Bible contains serious admonitions to churches that became blind and lost their way.

Linda's husband, Eric, says there are four ways of looking at the world: eyes closed frowning, eyes closed smiling, eyes open frowning, and eyes open smiling. We (Allan and Linda) have decided to open our eyes, see, and be seen in the context of God's church. This means listening to and acknowledging the whole body of Christ deeply. It is the posture of blessing: we bless one another when our eyes are open, even when our lips are shaped by an occasional frown. Mostly, however, we smile. We smile at the future and promise not to call you heretics too quickly when you experiment with new ways of living as the church, when you design new ways to live as God's people, when you embrace new metaphors and sing new songs. You are free, in the name of Jesus, to live in self-similarity to our Creator, free to embrace a participatory understanding of the nature of the Church, to trust God completely, leaning not on your own understanding, or for that matter on ours. Design, create, explore, and invent new ways to stomp out injustice, elevate the poor, cast out evil, care for the earth, and help people find their way into the arms of God. This is a day of blessing!

NOTES

Preface

1. *New York Times* archives (http://query.nytimes.com/gst/abstract .html?res=9D03EFDF1E39E633A25752C1A9679C946596D6CF), accessed Feb. 21, 2009.
2. Henry Ford and Samuel Crowther. *My Life and Work.* New York: Doubleday, Page, 1922, p. 72.
3. Ibid.
4. Lick-Wilmerding High School (http://www.lwhs.org), accessed Feb. 22, 2009.

Chapter One

1. Lewis Carroll. *Alice's Adventures in Wonderland.* (1865, chapter 5, p. 196 of *The Annotated Alice: Alice's Adventures in Wonderland & Through the Looking-Glass,* by Lewis Carroll, Martin Gardner, John Tenniel; illustrated by John Tenniel; contributor Martin Gardner; illustrated, annotated edition; New York: Norton, 2000).
2. http://www.thearda.com/quickstats; accessed Feb. 14, 2009.
3. Robert Greenleaf. *Servant Leadership: A Journey into the Nature of Legitimate Power and Greatness.* Mahwah, N.J.: Paulist Press, 1977, p. 299.
4. Daniel H. Williams, *Retrieving the Tradition and Renewing Evangelicalism: A Primer for Suspicious Protestants.* Grand Rapids, Mich.: Eerdmans, 1999), p. 9.

5. Brent Schendler, "Apple's 21st-Century Walkman CEO Steve Jobs thinks he has something pretty nifty. And if he's right, he might even spook Sony and Matsushita." Fortune, Nov. 12, 2001 (http://money.cnn.com/magazines/fortune/fortune_archive/2001/11/12/313342/index.htm); accessed Feb. 14, 2009.
6. Bruce Nussbaum. Quotes taken from a speech given at Innovation Night at the Royal College of Art in London and then written in his column, "CEOs Must Be Designers, Not Just Hire Them" (*Business Week,* June 28, 2007).
7. Alice Calaprice (ed.). *The Expanded Quotable Einstein.* Princeton, N.J.: Princeton University Press, 2000), p. 317. The actual quote is, "The significant problems we face cannot be solved at the same level of thinking we were at when we created them."
8. "Good Grief, Charlie Schulz!" *Time,* Jan. 1, 1965 (http://www.time.com/time/magazine/article/0,9171,841698,00.html); accessed Feb. 14, 2009.
9. "School: The Story of American Public Education." PBS series, Meryl Streep, narrator. This four-part series is about America's development of its public school systems since 1770.
10. Bill Gates. "America's High Schools Are Obsolete." Speech to the National Governor's Association, National Education Summit on High Schools, Feb. 26, 2005.
11. www.haroldbullock.com; accessed Feb. 14, 2009.
12. Unless otherwise indicated, all scriptural excerpts are from the New International Version (Colorado Springs: IBS-STL Global).
13. Frederick Engels, trans. by Emile Burns, *Anti Duhring: Herr Eugene Duhring's Revolution in Science* (1878), *Part I: Philosophy, IV. World Schematism* (Moscow: Progress, 1947), excerpts.
14. Calaprice (2000), p. 317.

Chapter Two

1. Parker Palmer. *Let Your Life Speak: Listening for the Voice of Vocation.* San Francisco: Jossey-Bass, 1999, p. 10.
2. 1 Peter 2:5.
3. Thomas Merton. *No Man Is an Island.* Orlando: Harcourt Trade, 2003, p. 168.
4. Exod. 20:8.
5. Speech at the Moe Work Plan Seminar, Ngee Ann Polytechnic Convention Center, Sept. 29, 2004.
6. Phil. 2:10–11.
7. 2 Cor. 12:7–10.

8. Brennan Manning. *The Ragamuffin Gospel*. Multnomah, CA: Multnomah Books, 1995, p. 26.
9. James Thurber, unsourced but widely and singularly attributed to him.
10. Peter Drucker. *The Essential Drucker: The Best of Sixty Years of Peter Drucker's Essential Writings on Management*. New York: HarperCollins, 2003, p. 218.
11. Alan J. Roxburgh and Fred Romanuk. *The Missional Leader: Equipping Your Church to Reach a Changing World*. San Francisco: Jossey-Bass, 2006, pp. 190ff.
12. Reggie McNeal. *Get a Life: It Really Is All About You*. Nashville: Broadman & Holman, 2007.
13. Ibid., p. 13.
14. Eric Johnson. *Foundations for Soul Care*. Downers Grove, IL: Inter-Varsity Press, 2007, p. 432.
15. "Vision and Expectations—Ordained Ministers in the Evangelical Lutheran Church in America." 1993 (http://www.elca.org/Growing-In-Faith/Vocation/Rostered-Leadership/Associates-in-Ministry/Vision-Expectations.aspx); accessed Feb. 21, 2009. This document was framed by Commissioned Associates in Ministry in the Evangelical Lutheran Church in America.
16. Michael Frost and Alan Hirsch. *The Shaping of Things to Come: Innovation and Mission for the 21st Century Church*. Peabody, Mass.: Hendrickson, 2003.
17. Hermann Hesse and Egon Schwartz. *Siddhartha, Demian, and Other Writings* (Ingrid Fry, ed.). London/New York: Continuum, 1992, p. 105.

Chapter Three

1. Fritjof Capra. *The Hidden Connections: A Science for Sustainable Living*. New York: Random House, 2002, p. 12.
2. Monica McGoldrick. *You Can Go Home Again: Reconnecting with Your Family*. New York: Norton, 1997, p. 101.
3. Charles Haddon Spurgeon. *Feathers for Arrows: Or, Illustrations for Preachers and Teachers, from My Note Book*. Oxford: Fleming H. Revell, 1870 (original from Oxford University), p. 41.
4. Frigyes Karinthy. *Chain Links*. Translated from Hungarian and annotated by Adam Makkai and Enikö Jankó.
5. Wendell Berry. "The Loss of the Future." *Religious Humanism*, (21)47, Nov. 20, 1968. This is from the concluding part of an article by Berry, which first appeared in the quarterly with copyright by the author (Box 278, Yellow Springs, OH 45387).

6. Edwy Plenel. "Ubuntu." *Humanist Declaration*. Le Monde (http://www.truthout.org/docs_05/010105H.shtml); accessed Dec. 1, 2008.
7. "The Micro Community; Why a Focus on Profitable Customers Might Be Shortsighted." (http://bizbrick.com/eretailnews/Features/0011microcommunity.htm); accessed Feb. 21, 2009.
8. Stephen J. Spignesi. *The Italian 100: A Ranking of the Most Influential Cultural, Scientific, and Political Figures, Past and Present*. New York: Citadel Press, 2003.
9. Clay Shirky. *Here Comes Everybody*. New York: Penguin Press, 2008, p. 197.
10. Henri Nouwen. "What Is Our Vision for Community?" (http://www.henrinouwen.org); accessed Feb. 21, 2009.
11. The Luke 10:2b prayer was conceived by Allan's mentor, Kenny Moore, and a friend. This was later documented in an article: Jim Montgomery, "Great Commission Update: Luke 10:2b Prayer" (Issue 2; http://lk10.com/index2.php?option=com_content&do_pdf=1&id=38); accessed February 11, 2009.
12. Michael Frost and Alan Hirsch. *The Shaping of Things to Come: Innovation and Mission for the 21st Century Church*. Peabody, Mass.: Hendrickson, 2003.
13. The International Mission Board of the Southern Baptist Convention recognizes this as a significant part of their definition in international settings.
14. Tim Chester and Steve Timmis. *Total Church: A Radical Reshaping Around Gospel and Community*. Wheaton, Ill.: Crossway Books, 2008, p. 56.

Chapter Four

1. Willa Cather. *Death Comes for the Archbishop*. New York: Random House, 1990, p. 50.
2. Stuart Murray. *Church Planting: Laying Foundations*. Peabody, Mass: Herald Press, 2001, p. 39.
3. SAET (The Society for the Advancement of Ecclesial Theology); http://www.saet-online.org; accessed Feb. 22, 2009.
4. Daniel H. Williams. *Retrieving the Tradition and Renewing Evangelicalism: A Primer for Suspicious Protestants*. Grand Rapids, Mich.: Eerdmans, 1999, p. 10.
5. GaryLamb.org, "Easter Egg Drop . . . The Rest of the Story" (http://www.garylamb.org/2008/03/26/easter-egg-dropthe-rest-of-the-story); accessed Feb. 22, 2009.
6. George Hunsberger. "Birthing Missional Faithfulness: Accents in a North American Movement." *International Review of Mission*,

Apr. 2003. Quoted from Missional Church Network, July 24, 2008, "Hunsberger & Missional Faithfulness" (http://missionalchurchnetwork .com/hunsberger-missional-faithfulness/).

7. REVEAL Teaser, Greg Hawkins (http://video.google.com/video search?client=safari&rls=en&q=willowCreek%20Greg%20Hawkins&i e=UTF-8&oe=UTF 8&um=1&sa=N&tab=wv#q=reveal%20Greg%20H awkins&emb=0); accessed Feb. 22, 2009.

8. Cathy Kirkpatrick, Mark Pierson, and Mike Riddell. *The Prodigal Project: Journey into the Emerging Church.* London: SPCK, 2003, p. 3.

9. Walter Bruggemann. *Cadences of Home: Preaching Among Exiles.* Louisville, Ky.: Westminster John Knox, 1997, p. 10.

10. Michael Frost. *Exiles: Living Missionally in a Post-Christian Culture.* Peabody, Mass.: Hendrickson, 2006, p. 8.

11. Stanley Hauerwas and William Willimon. *Resident Aliens.* Nashville: Abingdon Press, 1980, p. 69.

12. C. S. Lewis. *The Screwtape Letters.* (Originally published 1943.) Quoted from Walter Hooper in *C. S. Lewis: Complete Guide to His Life and Works.* New York: HarperCollins, 2005, p. 269.

13. *Scientific Autobiography and Other Papers,* trans. F. Gaynor (New York, 1949), pp. 33–34. As cited in T. S. Kuhn, *The Structure of Scientific Revolutions.* Chicago: University of Chicago, 1962.

14. Howard Snyder. *The Community of the King.* Downers Grove, Ill.: Inter-Varsity Press, 2004, p. 36.

Chapter Five

1. Darrell L. Guder and Lois Barrett (eds.). *Missional Church: A Vision for the Sending of the Church in North America.* Grand Rapids, Mich.: Eerdmans, 1998, p. 7.

2. Francis Schaeffer. *Pollution and the Death of Man: The Christian View of Ecology.* Wheaton, Ill.: Tyndale House, 1970, pp. 66–68.

3. Howard Snyder. *The Community of the King.* Downers Grove, Ill.: Inter-Varsity Press, 1978, p. 25.

4. Don Overstreet, church planter strategist, Southern California.

5. Rod Washington, Dieter Zander, Mark Scandrette, Ken McCord, and Dave Lantow.

6. Howard A. Snyder. *Liberating the Church: The Ecology of Church and Kingdom.* Downers Grove, Ill.: Inter-Varsity Press, 1983, p. 11.

7. Kirsteen Kim. "Mission Studies in Britain and Ireland: Introduction to a World-Wide Web." *British Journal of Theological Education,* Aug. 2000, *11*(1) (http://www.biams.org.uk/page.php?7); accessed Feb. 22, 2009.

8. Heinrich Kasting. *Toward the Twenty-First Century in Christian Mission: Essays in Honor of Gerald H. Anderson, Director, Overseas Ministries Study Center, New Haven, Connecticut, Editor*, International Bulletin of Missionary. Research by Gerald H. Anderson, James M. Phillips, Robert T. Coote (Grand Rapids, Mich.: Eerdmans, 1993), p. 177. Also in Kasting, trans. David Bosch, *Die Anfange der urchristlichen Mission* (1969); 127.

9. Aristotle, unsourced, but widely and singularly attributed to Aristotle.

Chapter Six

1. Wendell Berry. "The Loss of the Future." (Essay.) In *The Long-Legged House*. Berkeley, Calif.: Shoemaker & Hoard, 2004, p. 210.

2. The Karen tribe has become intimately important in the lives of the Karr family, who became legal guardians for three Karen teenagers in 2008 (Saymyahtoo, July, and Hosea). They also have become the "American parents" for several others who are in their early twenties (among them Margaret and Hsa K'Abru). As a result, Allan led a group of volunteers to start a new 501(c)(3), Ethne Global Services, serving as an agency helping internationals, especially refugees, find opportunities in America, particularly in education.

3. Percival Goodman and Paul Goodman. *Communitas: Means of Livelihood and Ways of Life*. Chicago: University of Chicago Press, 1947.

4. Alan Hirsch. *The Forgotten Ways: Reactivating the Missional Church*. Grand Rapids, Mich.: Brazos Press, 2006, p. 25.

5. Hirsch (2006), p. 24.

6. Hirsch (2006), p. 221.

7. Luke 10:2b is a common catch phrase now referring to a strategy of praying in pairs for people with a passion to be missionaries among a specific people group or area. No one knows for sure where it originated as first articulated, but this author personally believes it came from the heart of his mentor, Kenny Moore, and a friend, who wrote about it many years ago. The concept has spread like a virus.

8. Luke 11:13; our emphasis.

9. "Definition of Nidus." MedicineNet.com (http://www.medterms .com/script/main/art.asp?articlekey=10148); accessed Feb. 22, 2009.

10. Madeleine L'Engle. *The Irrational Season*. New York: Crosswicks, 1977, p. 158.

11. Paul Liberatore. "Churches Rally 400 in Marin Park Cleanup." *Marin Independent Journal* (http://www.marinij.com/marin/ci_ 8283054?source=email); accessed Feb. 22, 2009.

12. Wikipedia: Community portal (http://en.wikipedia.org/wiki/ Wikipedia:Community_portal); accessed Feb. 14, 2009.
13. Thomas Friedman. *The World Is Flat: A Brief History of the Twenty-First Century.* New York: Farrar, Straus, and Giroux, 2005.

Chapter Seven

1. "Church Organist Required for Jungle Meteorite Hunt." *Times Online* (http://www.timesonline.co.uk/tol/news/uk/science/ article1499849.ece); accessed Feb. 22, 2009.
2. "Church Organist."
3. "Explorer Cheats Death on Musical Mission." *Times Online* (http:// www.timesonline.co.uk/tol/news/world/us_and_americas/ article2267636.ece); accessed Feb. 22, 2009.
4. "Definition of Culture" (http://www2.eou.edu/~kdahl/cultdef.html); accessed Feb. 22, 2009.
5. David S. Dockery. *Renewing Minds: Serving Church and Society Through Christian Higher Education.* Nashville, Tenn.: B&H, 2007, p. 49.
6. James W. Sire. *Naming the Elephant: Worldview as a Concept.* Downers Grove, Ill.: Inter-Varsity Press, 2004, p. 161.
7. Dockery (2007), pp. 49–50.
8. Lausanne Committee for World Evangelization, Chicago meeting, 1982.
9. "Microculture." Dictionary.com (http://dictionary.reference.com/ browse/microculture); accessed Feb. 20, 2009.
10. "Indigenous." Definition from the Merriam-Webster Online Dictionary (http://www.merriam-webster.com/dictionary/indigenous); accessed Feb. 22, 2009.
11. "Adoniram Judson." *Wikipedia* (http://en.wikipedia.org/wiki/ Adoniram_Judson); accessed Feb. 22, 2009.
12. Alvin and Heidi Toffler. *Rethinking the Future: Rethinking Business Principles, Competition, Control and Complexity, Leadership, Markets and the World.* London/Boston: Rowan, Gibson, Nicholas Brealey, 1999, pp. viii ff.
13. "Indigenized." Dictionary.com (http://dictionary.reference.com/ browse/indigenized); accessed Feb. 22, 2009.
14. "Exegesis." Definition from the Merriam-Webster Online Dictionary (http://www.merriam-webster.com/dictionary/exegesis); accessed Feb. 22, 2009.
15. "Informant." Definition from the Merriam-Webster Online Dictionary (http://www.merriam-webster.com/dictionary/informant); accessed Feb. 22, 2009.

16. Paul A. Seaman, quoting David Pollock. *Global Nomads Washington Area (GNWA)* (http://www.globalnomads-dc.org/); accessed Feb. 20, 2009.
17. "Fareedzakaria.com" (http://fareedzakaria.com/index.html); accessed February 22, 2009.

Chapter Eight

1. Miroslav Volf. *Exclusion and Embrace: A Theological Exploration of Identity, Otherness, and Reconciliation.* Nashville: Abingdon, 1996, p. 51.
2. "Affinity." Definition from the Merriam-Webster Online Dictionary (http://www.merriam-webster.com/dictionary/affinity); accessed Feb. 22, 2009.
3. Christopher Alexander. *The Timeless Way of Building.* New York: Oxford University Press, 1979, p. 5.
4. Matt. 5:13–14 (The Message).
5. Paul G. Hiebert, R. Daniel Shaw, and Tite Tienou. Understanding Folk Religion. Grand Rapids, Mich.: Baker Books, 1999, p. 123.
6. Matt. 6:19–20.
7. Hiebert, Shaw, and Tienou (1999), p. 329.
8. Hiebert, Shaw, and Tienou (1999), p. 328.
9. Hiebert, Shaw, and Tienou (1999).
10. Hiebert, Shaw, and Tienou (1999).
11. Hiebert, Shaw, and Tienou (1999).

Chapter Nine

1. Vincent van Gogh. "The Letters: From Vincent to Theo, the Hague (I) 1882, c. 2 or 3 November 1882" (http://www.vggallery.com/letters/to_theo_netherlands_hague1.htm); accessed Feb. 22, 2009.
2. Paul Trachtman. "Van Gogh's Night Visions." *Smithsonian,* Jan. 2009, 71 (http://www.smithsonianmag.com/arts-culture/Night-Visions.html); accessed Feb. 22, 2009.
3. Allan Karr. "Protean Church." Academic convocation, presented Sept. 17, 2005. The Protean model is none of the models and all of the models at the same time. It allows the church to be grounded in biblical principles, empowered by the Holy Spirit, and dynamic and flexible to morph and evolve as the team is on journey together. This is an example of what designers might think about when they are considering a new design. In a business context, this means to be flexible but grounded in focus. "Protean" is descriptive of a church model which tenuously combines a foundational grounding

of the tenets of faith to Scripture while at the same time being fluid, diverse, and versatile, possessing the ability to "shape shift" according to the needs of the community and culture.
4. ethnechurch.net; accessed Jan. 15, 2009.

Chapter Ten

1. "Federico Fellini, Film Visionary, Is Dead at 73." *New York Times,* Nov. 1, 1993 (http://query.nytimes.com/gst/fullpage.html?res=9F0CE5DB1 53CF932A35752C1A965958260&partner=rssnyt&emc=rss); accessed Feb. 22, 2009.
2. "Starbucks: About Us." *Business Exchange* (http://bx.businessweek .com/starbucks/reference/); accessed Feb. 22, 2009.
3. Rutba House. *School(s) for Conversion: 12 Marks of a New Monasticism.* Eugene, Ore.: Cascade Books, 2005.
4. "Researchers Say Levees Had Design Flaws." USAToday.com (http:// www.usatoday.com/news/nation/2005–11–01-levee-flaws_x.htm); accessed Feb. 22, 2009.

Chapter Eleven

1. Bruce Nussbaum. "NussbaumOnDesign: Inside the Business of Innovation and Design." June 28, 2007. (http://www.businessweek .com/innovate/NussbaumOnDesign/archives/2007/06/ceos_ must_be_de.html); accessed on Feb. 21, 2009.
2. Tom Peters. *Re-imagine! Business Excellence in a Disruptive Age.* New York: DK, 2003, p. 134.
3. Peters (2003).
4. Jesse James Garrett. *The Elements of User Experience.* New York: American Institute of Graphic Arts, New Riders, 2003, pp. 22–23.
5. George Lakoff and Mark Johnson. *Metaphors We Live.* Chicago: University of Chicago Press, 1980, p. 158.
6. Gareth Morgan. *Images of Organization.* Thousand Oaks, Calif.: Sage, 2006. These descriptions are a synopsis of the metaphors around which Morgan has written an entire book.
7. Morgan (2006).
8. Samuel J. Palmisano (chairman, president, and chief executive officer, IBM). "The Enterprise of the Future." (Global CEO study.) 2008.
9. Howard Snyder. *The Problem of Wineskins.* Nottingham: Inter-Varsity Press Books, 1975.

Chapter Twelve

1. Georgia O'Keefe. *Full Bloom by Hunter Drohojowska*. New York: Norton, 2004, p. 103.
2. Rachel Carson. *The Sense of Wonder*. New York: Harper and Row, 1965, originally published 1956, p. 67.
3. Bruce Nussbaum. "'Innovation' Is Dead. Herald the Birth of 'Transformation' as the Key Concept for 2009." Posted Dec. 31, 2009, on BusinessWeek.com (http://www.businessweek.com/innovate/NussbaumOnDesign/archives/2008/12/innovation_is_d.html); accessed on Feb. 21, 2009.
4. Nussbaum (2009).
5. Nussbaum (2009).
6. Sheldon S. Wolin. *Politics and Vision: Continuity and Innovation in Western Political Thought*. Boston: Little, Brown, 1960, pp. 325–326.
7. Stewart Clegg, Cynthia Hardy, Thomas Lawrence, and Walter R. Nord. *The SAGE Handbook of Organizational Studies*. London: Sage, 2006, p. 19. Quote from Michael Reed, in the chapter "Organizational Theorizing: a Historically Contested Terrain."
8. Clegg, Hardy, Lawrence, and Nord (2006), p. 20.
9. J. W. Schulte Nordholt and Herbert H. Rowen. *Woodrow Wilson: A Life for World Peace*. Berkeley: University of California Press, 1991, p. 70.
10. Margaret J. Wheatley and Myron Kellner-Rogers. *A Simpler Way*. San Francisco: Berrett-Koehler, 1996, p. 2.
11. David J Bosch. *Transforming Mission: Paradigm Shifts in Theology of Mission*. New York: Orbis Books Maryknoll, 1998, p. 362.
12. Christopher Alexander. *A Timeless Way of Building*. New York: Oxford University Press, 1979, p. 368.
13. Frank Viola. *Reimagining Church: Pursuing the Dream of Organic Christianity*. Colorado Springs, Colo.: David C. Cook, 2008, p. 125.
14. Tom Peters. *Re-imagine! Business Excellence in a Disruptive Age*. London/New York: DK Adult, 2006, p. 152.
15. This is a core value for Eric Bergquist, director, Page Street Center, San Francisco.
16. William McDonough and Michael Braungart. *Cradle to Cradle: Remaking the Way We Make Things*. New York: North Point Press, 2002, p. 32.
17. "In Search of Good Food" (State of California's sustainable agriculture documentary). (http://insearchofgoodfood.blogspot.com/2009/01/resilience-vs-efficiency.html); accessed Feb. 14, 2009.
18. Linda Bergquist. "The Development of a Self-Help Manual for Sponsor Churches Working with Church Planters to Start New Mission Type Churches" (D.Min. Project, Golden Gate Baptist Theological Seminary, 2002), pp. 76–78. This content is adapted from Linda Bergquist's doctor of ministry project report.

ACKNOWLEDGMENTS

From Linda

One of my first memories of Eric Bergquist was the Wednesday evening he showed up at my church as an honored guest. Somehow he ended up flipping burgers for the crowd instead. I married that man, and I have been trying to learn Christ-centered humility from him ever since. He has been the love of my life and my best friend for twenty years. As the writing of this book comes to an end, I can hardly wait to start spending *much* more time with you, Eric. I am also indebted to my children, Harry and Kristina. Thank you both for forgiving me for not being completely present in your lives this past year. You have been wonderfully patient and understanding. And thank you, Kristina, for using your budding skills as a photographer to shoot the author photo we are using in this book. I am also grateful to my parents, Odd and Irene Solbakken, who raised me to believe that women can be smart, capable, and creative and can make a difference in the world.

Many of the ideas of this book were nurtured into being by the nonprofit organization ReImagine, in the days when it was a think tank. Thank you Dave and Marcia Lantow, Ken and Kellie McCord, Mark and Lisa Scandrette, Rod Washington, and Val and Dieter Zander, for your transparency and friendship during these ten amazing years.

I am also grateful to many from my church planting world: Golden Gate Seminary students, who have taught me as much as I teach them; committed strategists and church planters, who challenge me with their faithfulness; and my boss, Ross Shepherd, who represents the generous spirit of the California Southern Baptist Convention and the North American Mission Board. Thank you all for your encouragement and your trust in me. Blessings to you all!

From Allan

Along the journey of life, ministry, and the writing of this book, I have met many people I would now like to acknowledge. Foremost of these is Kathy, my partner in life and ministry. For twenty-three years, she has shown loyalty, joy, and patience as she encouraged me onward to joint achievements and milestones possible only with her partnership. Additionally, I would like to thank my family for consistently inspiring me and making me proud. Each of you gives my life joy and meaning. My family is a big group, starting with the four children born into our family: Josh, Alyssa, Hannah, and Micah. They form a foundation of joy and pride for me. Kathy and I are also legal guardians to three former refugees who are becoming well-educated Asian American young people: Saymyahtoo, July, and Hosea. They give my life great meaning. All of them generously and graciously shared time with "the book" while it was being written, and they provided many stories of life and ministry. Many other people share family status with them: parents, "adopted" children (Margaret, Tim, Hsa, and many others), and siblings. They all have contributed to the journey. Thanks!

I need to acknowledge many others. The people of Ethne Church Network are my church, my friends, ministry partners, and fellow travelers on the expedition of discovery. Kenny Moore serves as my faithful mentor, friend, prayer partner, reader, and volunteer editor. He faithfully prayed with me everyday, as did Jim Misloski, a friend, and former student, who also assisted with graphic designs for figures and charts in the book. You two men are rare gifts from God and are very appreciated.

Projects like a book are never created in a vacuum. Therefore, I would also like to thank my international friends who regularly hosted me in their homes, domestically and abroad, and who patiently taught me and answered my nosy questions. My students let me try out new ideas and thoughts, and they even verbally processed them in class. One student, Hans Edlund, generously helped me compile the Notes. Glory Dole helped as a reader. I would also like to thank my employers and colleagues at NAMB and Golden Gate Seminary, who encouraged me to write this book. Blessings to you all!

From Allan and Linda

We are both grateful to Alan Hirsch, not only for writing the Foreword to this book but for his passionately missional heart. Both of us have used his seminal writings as classroom texts, and God has also used those same texts to shape our ministries. Thank you, Alan, for honoring us with your contribution to this book and to our lives.

We are also indebted to our editors, Sheryl Fullerton and Julianna Gustafson, who patiently taught us how to write a book. They stretched us and encouraged us in new ways, and for that we are truly grateful. We also thank Leadership Network for trusting us to bear their name. What a privilege to be included in your list of authors!

We started this journey before we were even cognizant of it. God taught us along the way and introduced us to fellow travelers, including introducing us to one another along the way. We are learning how to be empowered and directed by the Holy Spirit. We are glad to have these words on paper, so we can now refocus from what we have learned in the past to what the future might hold.

ABOUT THE AUTHORS

Linda Bergquist works full-time as a church-starting strategist with the California Southern Baptist Convention and the North American Mission Board. She also works part-time as an adjunct professor at Golden Gate Baptist Theological Seminary. She holds a bachelor's degree in sociology from the University of California, San Diego; a master of divinity degree from Southwestern Baptist Theological Seminary; and a doctor of ministry degree from Golden Gate Baptist Theological Seminary. Linda has been involved in church planting for more than twenty-five years as a strategist, consultant, and teacher. She has lived in San Francisco with her husband, Eric, and daughter, Kristina, for thirteen years. Her son, Harry, lives and works in Canada. Eric directs the Page Street Baptist Center in San Francisco, where he engages in community transformation ministries along with many wonderful client volunteers. Linda selfishly supports Eric in this ministry whenever she can because it changes her for the better.

Allan Karr is a full-time professor at Golden Gate Baptist Theological Seminary and a national missionary with the North American Mission Board. He is a graduate of Oklahoma Baptist University and Midwestern Baptist Theological Seminary, and he earned his Ph.D. from Florida State University. For the past fifteen years, Allan and his family have been designing new churches and training others to do so, the last ten years as a professor and a mentor. He is passionate about his family, traveling abroad, construction projects, and community transformation by helping refugees. Allan lives in the mountain foothills outside Larkspur, Colorado, with his wife, Kathy, and their children, four by birth and three who were former refugees, and many others who regularly visit and consider themselves family. They use their home as an informal missional training center. This is his first book.

Index

Optimism, human-centered, 56–57
Organic churches, 135, 180
Organic, meaning of, 179–180, 182
Organisms: individuals as part of, 181; organizations as, 169, 180. *See also* Living systems; Living things
Organizational metaphors, 168–170
Organizational theory, historic juncture for, 179
Organizations: better, creating, 168–171; as organisms, 169, 180
Organizing: by design, 159–176; as living systems, 14–15, 180–182; new way of, 177–189
Organizing principles: congruency around, 147–156; described, 126–141; of our economy, 185
Ottoman Empire, 123
Outsiders: in groups related to Christian fellowship, *120*, 121; ministry team as, 104–107, 108; prophets as, 124
Overstreet, D., 71

P

Pacific Northwest, church subcultures in the, 122
Page Street Center Church, 92, 157, 184
Paid staff, issue of, 157
Pakistani people, 114, 142
Palmer, P., 17
Paradigm: efficiency, operating on the, issue of, 184–185; new, for the emerging world, 181–182; that is before us, considering the, 58–58; that is behind us, remembering the, 55–57
Paradigm shifts, 59–60, 177
Paradise Lost (Milton), 27
Parish model, 82
Partnerships, 156
Pastoral role, 43–44
Pathways Community Church, 42
Patterning mechanism, 61–63
Patterns: appreciating, 26; of behavior, fractal, 62, 72; that honor God, 52–66
Patton, S., 9
Paul, the Apostle, 26, 27, 40, 57, 62, 120, 121, 123, 153–154
Peace, cultural persons of, 110
Pentecostals, 139
People and place, ministry team loving the, importance of, 105

People group, meaning of, 100–101
People realm, *100*
Personal and team values, 152–153
Personal congruency, 155
1 Peter 2:5, 176
Peters, T., 161, 183
Pew Forum on Religion and Public Life, 55
Philippi, 116
Philippians 1:1, 116
Philippians 3:10, 69
Pierson, M., 55
Place and people, ministry team loving the, importance of, 105
Planck, M., 60
Pluralistic societies, 101
Postmodernism, 4, 58
Practical congruency, 153–154
Practical considerations: for attractional churches, 134; example of, in determining a church model, 142; for relational churches, 138
Practice-oriented, 67
Pragmatic alignment, *166*
Prayer: common, capacity for, 39; and releasing communitas, 83–88
"Prayer Discipleship," 84–86
Prayer movement, 40, 83, 196n7
Predictability, 21
"Present tense" vs. "present/future tense" mission, 76–77
Present, the: gap connecting, to the future, living in the, 3; sustaining, task of, 3–5
Priests, leadership role of, 124
Programs, missions, vs. missional theology, 75–76
Progress, idea of, 57
Protean model, 143–144, 198–199n3
Protestant minority, U.S. becoming a, 55
Protestantism, in the Enlightenment era, 57
Proverbs 1:5, 107
Psalm 148:1–5, 71
Public education system: critique of, 9, 10; redesigning the, 11; in Singapore, 22–23
Purpose-driven churches, 131, *148*

Q

Quantitative measures, issue of, 56
Quantum physics, shift to, 59–60
QWERTY keyboard, 51, 52